RESTAURANT REPUBLIC

RESTAURANT REPUBLIC

The Rise of Public Dining in Boston

Kelly Erby

A Quadrant Book

UNIVERSITY OF MINNESOTA PRESS
MINNEAPOLIS · LONDON

Quadrant, a joint initiative of the University of Minnesota Press and the Institute for Advanced Study at the University of Minnesota, provides support for interdisciplinary scholarship within a new, more collaborative model of research and publication.

QUADRANT

http://quadrant.umn.edu

Sponsored by the Quadrant Design, Architecture, and Culture group (advisory board: John Archer, Ritu Bhatt, Marilyn DeLong, Greg Donofrio, and Katherine Solomonson) and by the College of Design at the University of Minnesota.

Quadrant is generously funded by the Andrew W. Mellon Foundation.

The University of Minnesota Press gratefully acknowledges financial assistance for the publication of this book from the Department of History at Washburn University.

Copyright 2016 by the Regents of the University of Minnesota

All rights reserved. No part of this publication may be reproduced, stored in a retrieval system, or transmitted, in any form or by any means, electronic, mechanical, photocopying, recording, or otherwise, without the prior written permission of the publisher.

Published by the University of Minnesota Press
111 Third Avenue South, Suite 290
Minneapolis, MN 55401-2520
http://www.upress.umn.edu

Printed in the United States of America on acid-free paper

The University of Minnesota is an equal-opportunity educator and employer.

22 21 20 19 18 17 16   10 9 8 7 6 5 4 3 2 1

Library of Congress Cataloging-in-Publication Data
Names: Erby, Kelly, author.
Title: Restaurant republic : the rise of public dining in Boston / Kelly Erby.
Description: Minneapolis, MN : University Of Minnesota Press, 2016. | Series: A quadrant book | Includes bibliographical references and index.
Identifiers: LCCN 2016014255 | ISBN 978-0-8166-9130-2 (hc) | ISBN 978-0-8166-9131-9 (pb)
Subjects: LCSH: Restaurants—Massachusetts—Boston—History—19th century. | Dinners and dining—Social aspects—Massachusetts—Boston—History—19th century. | Food habits—Massachusetts—Boston—History—19th century. |
Boston (Mass.)—Social conditions—19th century. | BISAC: HISTORY / Social History. | HISTORY / United States / 19th Century. | HISTORY / United States / State & Local / New England (CT, MA, ME, NH, RI, VT).
Classification: LCC TX909.2.M32 B674 2016 | DDC 647.95744/61—dc23
LC record available at https://lccn.loc.gov/2016014255

To my parents,
MARK *and* KATHY ERBY

Contents

INTRODUCTION Dining Out in Boston   ix

1 Filet de Boeuf at the Tremont House
Luxury Hotel Dining Rooms   1

2 Bolted Beef and Bolted Pudding
Eating Houses   43

3 Charlotte Russe in the Afternoon
Elite Ladies' Eateries   63

4 Roast, Chop Suey, and Beer
Cafés   83

EPILOGUE Ice Cream at Howard Johnson's   107

Acknowledgments   111

Notes   115

Index   143

INTRODUCTION

Dining Out in Boston

In May 1857, Benjamin Crowninshield, a Harvard student from an affluent Boston family, purchased some raw oysters from a shop near Quincy Market and ate them with his friend John. He referred to this late-afternoon activity as "oystering." Two days later, Crowninshield enjoyed a dish of ice cream with a female friend at a local confectioner's shop. He began the next week by meeting classmates for supper at the Parker House Hotel, one of Boston's preeminent dining spots, with a menu consisting largely of fashionable French cuisine. Tuesday found Crowninshield back at Parker's for his afternoon meal, as did Wednesday. On Friday, Class Day at Harvard, Crowninshield stopped again for oysters at Lyon's Oyster Saloon in Cambridge. This time, he ate the bivalves for breakfast, not an uncommon morning meal in those days when Americans' desire for oysters was almost insatiable. And, after participating in the festivities at Harvard, Crowninshield once more met friends at Parker's where he ate so much that, as he confided to his diary, "I had to relieve myself by inserting my fingers in my throat till my stomach came up."[1]

This snapshot of one Bostonian's springtime dining activities is reflective of just how commonplace dining out had become in urban America by the mid-nineteenth century. Crowninshield, young and privileged, was able to partake of some of the finest restaurants in Boston and clearly overindulged on at least this one occasion. But it was not just the elite who participated in the new urban trend of commercial dining. By the 1850s in cities like Boston, there was a dining venue to fit every taste and pocketbook.

THE BROAD SHIFT TO COMMERCIAL DINING

Dining commercially had not always been such a common part of urban life. Throughout the colonial and early national periods, Americans hardly ever ate outside the home. Taverns supplied potluck meals to travelers and hosted the occasional political or civic banquet. But, as a rule, patrons imbibed at their local taverns, and shared the newspaper, or read the latest political pamphlets; they did not usually eat full meals.[2] There was not often a reason to do so, since home was rarely far away. In these years, there was not yet a clear demarcation between domestic and work spaces, and urban centers were relatively small and easily traversable by foot. For example, Boston, the focus of this study, was still just a spidery peninsula with most of the population living and working within a two-mile radius.[3] Meanwhile, travel to any great distance was a long, arduous, and expensive process, and not often undertaken.[4] As a result, commercial dining options in early America, in contrast to many larger European cities, were strictly limited.[5]

But by the 1820s, the heightened pace of economic activity and early stages of industrialization that historians refer to as the market revolution had begun to cause broad and deep disruptions to the texture of

John Marshall, *Boston et Ses Environs*, 1807. David Rumsey Historical Map Collection.

American life, disruptions that would have major consequences for dining patterns in Boston and other urban areas.[6] The port town of Boston, long an entrepôt for goods imported from abroad and American agricultural products intended for export, now also became a hub for manufactured items like shoes and textiles arriving from Massachusetts's rural hinterlands. Boston businessmen invested heavily in the surrounding new factory towns. The capital they amassed helped to make Boston itself (incorporated as a city in 1822) a powerful financial center, second only to New York by 1830.[7]

Manufacturing and industry within the city of Boston developed somewhat late but flourished in the decades on either side of the Civil War. This efflorescence was due, in large part, to the arrival of the Irish after 1845. Tens of thousands of deeply impoverished Irish immigrants, willing to work for any wage, flooded Boston and supplied the cheap labor force that made the factory system and the expansion of the heavy industries possible.[8]

Scores of new manufactories, from shoe and clothing makers to iron and brass foundries, opened their doors. Older, dying industries like sugar refining were also suddenly revitalized through a combination of new mechanized technologies and access to inexpensive labor. The number of industrial employees in Boston doubled between 1845 and 1855; it doubled again between 1855 and 1865.[9] Within two decades, Boston became the country's fourth-largest manufacturing city. At the same time, small-scale shop production thrived in Boston, invigorated by the influx of commerce and population. The economy further hosted a variety of nonmanufacturing activities, including casual male labor along streets and docks and domestic work, the latter especially for women.

Overall, the city bustled. Immigrants from other areas of Great Britain, as well as from Germany, France, Poland, Switzerland, Italy, and, later, China joined the Irish in Boston (though in considerably smaller numbers) to take advantage of new opportunities there.[10] The total population exploded, jumping from just over 43,000 in 1820 to almost 140,000 by 1850. Geographic boundaries likewise steadily expanded. And facilitated by a new network of canals, steamboats, and railroads, thousands of businessmen and tourists visited Boston each year.[11]

These transformations created steadily increasing and widespread demand for commercial dining options in Boston.[12] To start with, Boston's

Robert Salmon, *View of Boston Harbor*, 1843. Oil on panel, 9 5/8 × 11 5/8 inches. Private collection.

elite began demanding new kinds of public venues in which to meet one another or to fete the city's many guests and important visitors. At the same time, as work moved out of the home, the growing number of men toiling in factories or offices found it more convenient to purchase and eat their midday meal from commercial establishments close to their workplace rather than return home to dine. In the antebellum years, because of the limited and less public occupations to which they were largely restricted, female employees were less likely to need commercial refreshment. But the number of women workers seeking to dine out in the afternoon increased as their employment prospects broadened through the course of the century.[13] Meanwhile, as more affluent middle-class and elite women assumed roles as the primary consumers for their families, and as they became more involved in civic and social organizations, they too relied on restaurants near their favorite downtown stores and meeting spots.[14] Theater- and concertgoers began incorporating restaurants into their pursuit of commercial entertainment.[15] In fact, dining out became its own form of entertainment and restaurants another kind of urban space where elite Bostonians could both see and be seen. On the other end of the social spectrum, the cramped living conditions of many residents—thanks to the city's chronic housing shortage—led tenement dwellers, boardinghouse occupants, and lodgers to seek out eateries for socializing as much as for sustenance.[16] Finally, immigrants who had settled in Boston from all over the world, particularly the many bachelors, patronized restaurants owned by others from their homelands that offered tastes of the old world in the new. Boston's dining landscape continued to grow and change throughout the century, along with the city itself.

SEGMENTATIONS IN SOCIETY, CULTURE, AND DINING OUT

The same market developments that made commercial dining a broad trend in Boston, however, also created a more fragmented, hierarchical society with sharper demarcations among class, race, and ethnic groups. This too shaped how Bostonians dined, leading to the creation of a highly segmented dining landscape.

Overall, the city's commercial and professional sectors prospered as a result of Boston's economic expansion, advancing the upper and middle classes. These constituencies were most likely to be white, native-born Americans. Unskilled and semiskilled workers, on the other hand—more than half the city's workforce by 1850—fell further and further behind in terms of wealth accumulation over the course of the century.[17]

The large numbers of Irish immigrants and the small but growing population of African Americans in Boston faced the greatest impediments to social and economic mobility. Both groups were relied on for their cheap labor, but each faced limited resources and severe discrimination due to ethnic and racial prejudices against them. Throughout the antebellum period, they were typically restricted to the lowest paying, least esteemed, and most dangerous kinds of employment the city offered and were the least likely to achieve meaningful socioeconomic advancement.[18] Later in the century, discrimination against Irish Bostonians lessened as a result of shifting racial paradigms. Unfortunately, these same ideas further heightened prejudice toward the increasing number of Southern and Eastern Europeans, as well as toward those of African and Asian descent.[19] Boston's brief but reoccurring economic downturns throughout the 1800s unfailingly hurt these already marginalized members of society the most. Economic mobility was certainly possible in Boston, but overall the gaps in wealth and opportunity between rich and poor, native-born and immigrant, white and nonwhite widened steadily across the century.

The physical distance between different constituencies grew as well. Beginning in the late eighteenth century, Boston had laboriously begun work on several landfill projects that gradually expanded the size of the peninsula and slowly allowed the growing population to fan out across it to areas like the West End and Beacon Hill.[20] At the same time, improvements in transportation systems made surrounding suburbs like Roxbury, Brighton, and Dorchester more accessible.[21] Affluent Bostonians steadily escaped the increasingly commercial North End and central business district to live in these less crowded regions, which the city incorporated in the years after the Civil War. Later landfill projects transformed the Back Bay and new South End into additional habitable space, leaving Boston a sprawling metropolis of more than thirty-six square miles by 1880.[22]

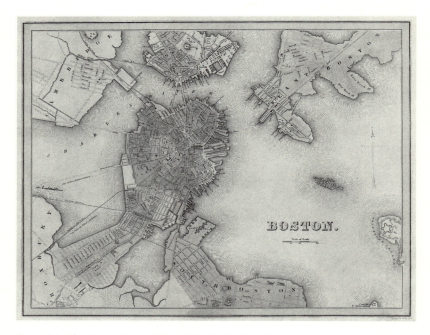

Thomas G. Bradford, *Boston*, 1841. David Rumsey Historical Map Collection.

Meanwhile, the overwhelming number of Boston's working-class and poorer residents, unable to afford commuting costs, continued to live clustered in the city's North End, close to employment at the docks and factories. Here was the origin of Boston's slums. Once fine but now dilapidated mansions were carved up into tenements to make room for the mushrooming immigrant population while additional "sheds and shanties" were thrown up in every available space between.[23] Another sordid quarter of nineteenth-century Boston was the area just behind the

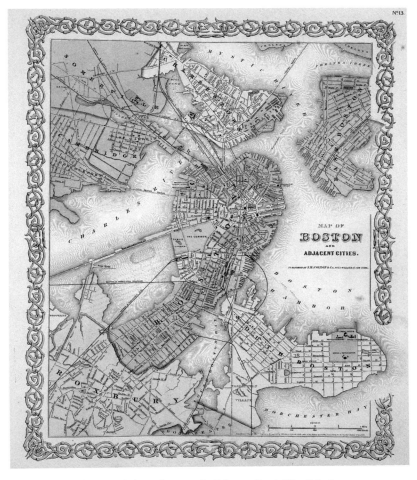

G. W. Colton, *Map of Boston and Adjacent Cities*, 1856. David Rumsey Historical Map Collection.

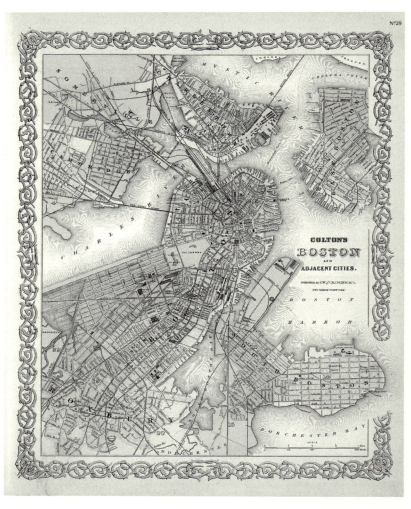

G. W. Colton, *Boston and Adjacent Cities,* 1886. Note the significant change in the geographic size and shape of Boston since 1807, thanks to a series of landfill projects completed during the century. David Rumsey Historical Map Collection.

West End, known as "Nigger Hill," where more than half of Boston's black population (as well as some poor whites) resided.[24] Neighborhoods in Boston continued to evolve throughout the 1800s. By late in the century, the formerly white and genteel South and West Ends had taken on thoroughly working-class qualities, as had South Boston where new factories provided growing employment opportunities.[25] Within these areas there were distinct enclaves of Irish, Italian, Chinese, blacks, and Jews. The white and affluent meanwhile continued to filter out to surrounding suburbs, building fine new homes and relying on public transportation to commute back to the city each day for work, shopping, or civic engagements.

These multiplying and deepening divisions between Boston residents were reflected in the city's growing commercial dining options. Bostonians from all backgrounds participated in the trend toward dining out. But different constituencies throughout the 1800s patronized different eateries, where they engaged in different dining rituals through which they signaled their own unique values, tastes, and identities. Factors such as location, décor, level of service, cost, and type and quality of fare all served to distinguish dining establishments and attract specific clienteles, clienteles that then added their own unique flavors to venues through their dress and behaviors. Boston soon hosted an expansive but stratified spectrum of eateries. From sophisticated downtown hotel dining rooms specializing in trendy French cuisine to cheap basement eating houses near the wharves and factories, from refined ladies' confectioners to North End Italian tables d'hôte and the Chinese "chop chop sue" houses scattered along Harrison Avenue, there were soon as many restaurants in Boston as there were appetites.

EXAMINING THE DIVERSE RESTAURANT LANDSCAPE

In *Restaurant Republic: The Rise of Public Dining in Boston,* I examine the nascent restaurant landscape in Boston in its entirety, from the most plebeian of eateries to the extremely elite and refined. Focusing on the rise of commercial dining in one specific city allows me to systematically explore the varied networks of public dining venues that catered to distinct groups of urbanites. Historical attention to American foodways has peaked in recent decades, but no existing work provides such a comprehensive account of the early decades of commercial dining in this country.[26]

The story of why Americans embraced dining out and the wide variety of ways in which they began to do so is an important one. Restaurants were a major part of a growing trend in urban public venues dedicated to consumer leisure in the nineteenth century.[27] Along with theaters, department stores, and hotels, restaurants provided a public stage at a time when, still fresh from their revolution, Americans were eager to enter into the public sphere and define themselves as a people.[28] But perhaps more than these other public commercial spaces, restaurants were also sharply differentiated. Thus the study of restaurant dining in this period provides an opportunity to cast new light on how Americans attempted to balance the revolutionary ideal of egalitarianism against a growing capitalist consumer culture that both reflected and contributed to social hierarchy.

The mounting number of public dining establishments during the nineteenth century as well as the varieties of types attest to the growing number of people participating in public eating. Dining away from home then became part of a shared urban culture in which most, if not all, city dwellers began to engage. And, in theory at least, any hungry Bostonian could take a seat at any restaurant and order a meal. Surely such accessibility signaled the achievement of equality in American society.

Or did it? The reality was that bolting down a plate of greasy hash at an eating house did not carry the same cultural meaning as feasting on a multicourse meal at a luxury hotel dining room.[29] Moreover, a wide range of factors shaped and limited who dined where, including what the venue cost, the kinds of foods it served, the level of decorum it demanded of its customers, and the degree of gender, racial, and ethnic diversity it tolerated. Thus, while dining out was a common experience urbanites shared in the nineteenth century, it was also a trend characterized by the fragmentation and difference that historians have demonstrated increasingly defined America's urban, market-driven society.[30]

On the other hand, this book also uncovers some surprising ways in which the experience of dining out could provide opportunities for cultural experimentation, transmission, and fusion. As young bon vivant Benjamin Crowninshield's dining patterns suggest, Bostonians could—and did—vary the expense and quality of their restaurant choices, dining higher up in the hierarchy of restaurants on some occasions and eating lower on the spectrum on others. To be sure, not all Bostonians had the same freedom in where they dined, since not everyone could afford to patronize elite venues like Parker's, and not every restaurant welcomed women, African Americans, or immigrants. Still, even restaurants that excluded racial and ethnic minorities as customers often hired them as employees. Indeed, restaurants were one of a limited number of inter-racial workplaces in the nineteenth century. Moreover, the diversity of foods and dining behaviors on display in the city's restaurants soon provoked interest (though sometimes also repulsion) among Bostonians. Their curiosity and appetites whetted, Bostonians began crossing comestible boundaries. Thus, while the city itself was full of cultural differences and divided by economic and social change in this period, *Restaurant Republic* reveals an emergent nineteenth-century dining landscape that reflected but also crosscut socioeconomic, gender, racial, and ethnic affiliations.

Unfortunately, the political consequences of the culinary pluralism that restaurants facilitated were limited. Chapter 1 discusses the respect that wealthy, white Bostonians came to hold for the significant number of black waiters who served them in the city's luxury dining venues, for example; however, the admiration these Bostonians felt for their waiters' considerable skill did not mean that they also supported enhanced occupational opportunities for blacks. In fact, the occupational discrimination that blacks continued to face in Boston throughout the century explained why so many African American men worked as waiters in the first place. Likewise, chapter 4 finds that at least some white, native-born Bostonians became open to trying Chinese food late in the century. But this did not mean that they also supported lifting the Chinese Exclusion Act. To the contrary, Chinese food probably only found the limited popularity it did among white Bostonians in this period because the Chinese Exclusion Act was in place, thus curbing the Chinese "threat" and helping to make white Americans feel comfortable visiting Chinese restaurants to try Chinese food.[31]

The nineteenth-century American experience, as many historians have demonstrated, tilted toward democratization but also toward hierarchical segmentation.[32] Public dining, as this book demonstrates, is unique for its insight into each of these divergent trends, as well as for its centrality to both. Dining commercially offered Bostonians a unifying culture even as that culture became increasingly diverse.

WHY BOSTON?

I devote my full attention in *Restaurant Republic* to the trend of dining out in a specific nineteenth-century metropolis. Boston was certainly not the only city in America to develop a highly variegated dining landscape during the nineteenth century; on the contrary, a similar process occurred to some degree in nearly every urban center in the Northeast. So why does Boston in particular provide the location for my case study? Or to phrase the question the way it is has often been asked of me during the course of this project: why isn't New York, America's "greatest restaurant city," my focus instead? Indeed, the New York dining scene far surpassed Boston's in magnitude and diversity, even in the nineteenth century. I have chosen to concentrate on Boston in part precisely because it is not New York. During the 1800s, New York became, by a considerable margin, the largest, most diverse American metropolis and the acknowledged restaurant capital of the country.[33] By comparison, Boston's more modest assortment of restaurants, its less impressive—but still significant—expansion in commerce and population, and its growing demographic diversity made it more typical of other urban centers in the United States. And yet the attention paid to New York dining fashions by modern critics and scholars (and even by nineteenth-century contemporaries) has tended to obscure the understanding of American appetites outside of New York. This book strives to correct that imbalance.

At the same time, the ways in which Boston was atypical compared to other U.S. cities further distinguish the city as an ideal case study. For one, Boston's leaders envisioned the city as the cultural bellwether of America.[34] This leadership actively strove to realize in Boston its dream of a well-ordered republic that fostered cultural and humanitarian values. As a result, Boston was deeply conservative in some respects, resistant to social change and anxious about growing social and cultural fragmentation. But the heightened consideration to these matters also cultivated a climate of debate in Boston regarding the complex issues of class, race, immigration, and culture. When it came to food, what the citizens of the young republic ate and how they ate it seems to have mattered more in Boston than in other cities, a fact that has helped in illuminating issues of interest to this project that are not as obvious in other communities. Many prominent Bostonians, for example, were early and strong

Introduction

supporters of Sylvester Graham, the antebellum dietary reformer who aimed to help Americans negotiate the rapid changes of market society by advocating they avoid commercialized foods and instead idealizing home food production and plain living.[35] Indeed, the American Physiological Society, a national diet reform organization established on Graham's diet principles, was founded in Boston in 1837.[36] Likewise, Boston was home to the Boston Cooking School and New England Kitchen, postbellum organizations that aimed in part to use food as a vehicle through which to assimilate immigrants to American society.[37]

BOSTON'S RESTAURANTS

My approach in this book is primarily thematic. Each chapter explores one of the most common genres of restaurants in nineteenth-century Boston: elite hotel dining rooms, male-dominated eating houses, ladies' dining rooms and confectioners, and mixed-gender cafés. I examine the general locations of each of these kinds of venues, their characteristic décor and cuisine, and the economic, ethnic, and racial backgrounds of their clientele. I do my best, using a wide variety of sources (including menus, newspaper articles and advertisements, city directories, guidebooks, and diaries) to re-create the meals and social interactions experienced in these dining establishments and the functions these venues served in the lives of their patrons. I investigate how the different eateries influenced each other and changed over time, while also considering the larger social and cultural consequences of the entire spectrum of dining establishments in Boston. I further consider the function of restaurants as workplaces for kitchen staff and waiters and as business ventures for proprietors. My study begins with the origins of dining out in Boston in the late 1820s and concludes in the decades after the Civil War, when the transformation of Boston to its own form of a "restaurant city" was complete.

Boston's wealthy elite were the first to demand new kinds of public dining options, and so my study begins with the venues this elite sought out and patronized. Though Americans had been scornful of European cultural models as enervating and corrupting, wealthy Bostonians increasingly looked to French modes for inspiration when it came to sophisticated dining. This was especially surprising given Federalist Boston's previous antagonism to the French. In the 1820s, Boston's upper class, in their role as "patrons of culture," organized the construction of the Tremont House in Boston. The main attraction of this Boston institution was its dining room and the opulent, heavily French-influenced cuisine it produced. In chapter 1, I examine the Tremont House and other luxurious public dining rooms (including young bon vivant Benjamin Crowninshield's beloved Parker House) that soon competed with the Tremont for elite patronage. In such venues, the Boston elite demonstrated themselves to be republican aristocracy and strove to enact social and cultural codes that would hopefully stabilize society. But these very codes also underscored and in some ways facilitated fluidity and mobility and thus undermined social and cultural hierarchies.

As economic opportunities in Boston continued to proliferate and diversify, men in various occupations—from factory workers to bankers—turned to eateries to provide convenience meals during the workday. In chapter 2, I consider Boston's eating houses, which all aimed to provide straightforward noontime meals to men in a hurry. But there were many grades of eating houses, each catering to a different economic class of male diner. Class was also tied importantly to ethnic and racial difference. Distinctions in location, décor, service, and menu among various eating houses were all central to the standing of the patrons that a particular establishment attracted and significantly shaped a customer's dining experience. At the same time, all eating houses helped to construct new notions of urban masculinity and contributed to the creation of a more consumer-oriented society.

Most nineteenth-century dining venues, including eating houses, were male spaces and typically inaccessible to women. But middle- and upper-class women, through their expanding roles as the main consumers for their families and their participation in women's associations and reform activities, increasingly found themselves downtown in the middle of the day and in need of dining options of their own. In chapter 3, I turn to the growing number of dining establishments earmarked specifically for respectable, affluent women. These ladies' dining venues strove to uphold mainstream gender ideals and distinguish themselves as appropriate for female use through their location, décor, and menu, all gendered as feminine. Nevertheless, by providing semipublic space for women to patronize, ladies' eateries helped to draw women into the public sphere, thus posing a fundamental challenge to gender norms. The public and commercial dining activities of respectable women also became a vehicle for the discussion of anxieties associated with the rise of consumer pleasure more generally.

In the last decades of the century, as shifting mealtimes successfully postponed the main meal until after the workday was complete, a wider range of mixed-gender cafés opened that specialized in providing more relaxed evening meals to working- and middle-class Bostonians eager to take advantage of new opportunities for commercialized leisure. Many establishments, owned by the city's now even more heterogeneous population of immigrants, specialized in "ethnic" or foreign foods, fostering ethnic-class enclaves within the larger urban environment. Indeed, opening a restaurant represented an entrée to entrepreneurship and an avenue of economic mobility for immigrant proprietors. As I show in chapter 4, the city's growing assortment of ethnic restaurants helped to expose Bostonians of all backgrounds to new tastes and dining rituals. Throughout the nineteenth century, Boston's restaurants thus contributed to a dynamic consumer-oriented public culture and shaped a new understanding of the role of difference in American society and culture.

CHAPTER I

Filet de Boeuf at the Tremont House

Luxury Hotel Dining Rooms

The Tremont House opened in Boston on October 16, 1829, with a celebratory dinner held in the hotel's lavishly decorated public dining room. Of the city's prominent merchants and political leaders, 120 attended this occasion. Guests seated around the Tremont's magnificently carved walnut banquet table included U.S. Senator Daniel Webster, U.S. Representative Edward Everett, Supreme Court Justice Joseph Story, and Boston's mayor Josiah Quincy, who presided over the affair. The men feasted on a succession of forty-four dishes, served in five different courses, each and every one of them "costly delicacies skillfully prepared" and delivered from the kitchen by an interracial staff of waiters. Newspapers reported the dinner was "in all respects tasteful and elegant," with a sizeable portion of the fare consisting of French cuisine, "the perfection of cookery." Numerous toasts were offered congratulating and commending Boston for the civic and cultural achievement it had attained in building the Tremont House, the country's most elegant dining establishment. The revelers also raised a glass several times during the meal to the "skillful, honest, and honorable mechanics of Boston," who had helped to erect the Tremont. Doctor Everett in particular spoke at length about how the successful construction of the Tremont, which had required the cooperation of several different "pursuits"—both merchants (who had helped raise the staggering $3,000,000 necessary for the venture) and mechanics (who had built it)—was a metaphor for the "well-constituted" nature of American society itself. The noble tradesmen of whom he spoke, the "perfect complement" to the merchants seated around the table, however, were notably absent from the dinner commemorating the hotel's completion.[1]

The Tremont House revolutionized dining in Boston and throughout America. Its public—but expensive—dining room, open to both hotel guests and Boston's local elite, transformed what had once been a more or less straightforwardly biological act, eating, into the height of luxury in America. What is more, the Tremont commercialized dining and made it part of the public sphere. In the years immediately following its opening, Boston—like other major U.S. cities of the Northeast—experienced an explosion in commercial dining options as eating out became an integral part of urban life. Not all venues offered the same opulent experience the Tremont did; however, the hotel set an important precedent for future restaurants in the way it functioned as a stage on which its affluent patrons defined their cultural values and endeavored to cement their authority through a public display of consumption, ritual, and taste.[2]

TAVERN DAYS

To fully appreciate the departure the opening of the Tremont House in 1829 represented, it is important to first sketch out some of Boston's early history pertaining to public eating and drinking. This history begins with taverns. Taverns were among the earliest American businesses, providing shelter and community to colonial settlers eking out a civilization in the wilderness.[3] In colonial Massachusetts, the government attempted to restrict public drinking by requiring that taverns licensed to sell alcohol also be equipped to provide lodging and meals to travelers. In other words, a *tavern* was also required to be an *inn*; the two terms were even used interchangeably.[4] These regulations remained in place until 1832. The primary trade of most Massachusetts taverns, however, was the sale of alcohol to local men, who gathered at taverns to socialize, obtain news, and conduct business and politics. Due to associations between commercial alcohol and commercial sex, respectable women avoided taverns except in the relatively unlikely event that they were traveling, rare for women until well into the nineteenth century.

The sale of food was tangential to the business of tavern keeping. Generally speaking, only travelers sought meals at early Boston taverns, and then it was out of necessity and not choice. Tavern keepers hardly put much thought into the fare they provided; they just wanted to feed their lodgers the meals for which they had already paid and which they as licensed tavern keepers were required to supply. Most tavern keepers lived in their taverns along with their families, and it was usually the tavern keeper's wife who prepared lodgers' meals. Lodgers typically also ate with the family, enjoying no additional fanfare than what normally accompanied a family meal. Robert, a traveler in early-national New England, described a dinner at one tavern where he stayed:

> The table was spread, with a dirty cloth, and half a dozen children, bedaubed from ear to ear with candy and dirt, hung around it, pulling at the bread, and hauling the dishes out of place. The good hostess . . . presently entered with a plate of sausages, her hair . . . occasionally swept in charming negligence through the gravy.[5]

Tavern meals like this one were served only at regular, predetermined times. If a lodger missed the midday "dinner," the largest meal of the day throughout most of American history and typically served between noon and three, he went without it.

The clientele of most early American taverns was extraordinarily democratic, with rich and poor, free and bound, black and white mixing at the public bar.[6] But beginning in the mid-eighteenth century, some proprietors sought to capitalize on an expansion of wealth in the colonies, swelling urban populations, and an increasing number of travelers by upgrading the quality of their accommodations to appeal specifically to a higher class of clientele. Those who wanted to distinguish their businesses from a traditional tavern (and demand a higher rent) moved into larger, grander buildings—typically former private mansions—with space for the banquets and balls of elite local society, as well as rooms for overnight guests. Many began using the more sophisticated French word *hôtel* to describe their businesses (though the use of this word could be misleading as many ordinary taverns began to adopt it as well).[7]

Greater consideration was also given to provisions. Meals were still included in the price of board and provided at set times, but instead of meals served family style, guests at the best hotels now gathered in large dining rooms to feast on what could include as many as ten to sixteen different dishes. Indeed, the best early American hotels staked their reputations on the abundance and variety of their daily afternoon dinners, or "ordinaries." At a single meal, options might include venison, bear steaks, wild duck, wild turkey, lobster, terrapin, salmon, oysters, pork, and mutton. Desserts ranged from plum pudding to apple pies and cranberry tarts. This food was laid out on a large table and guests were expected to help themselves to whatever—and as much—as they wanted. The proprietor himself carved the meat as a sign of his generous hospitality.[8]

And yet, even at the nicest hotels the fare was plentiful, but the experience was not particularly special. The dishes were almost always the same standard British American fare long prevalent throughout New England.[9] Guests frequently complained that this food was not cooked well; the meat was stringy or greasy, and the pastries soggy. Who knew how long this food had been sitting out prior to mealtime? Usually everything was served at room temperature. Nor was there anything unique about the way the fare was presented, heaped upon a table. For their part, most hotel diners were hardly on their best behavior when they entered the dining room. On the contrary, dinner was a mad dash to lay claim to the best viands on the table and to eat as much as possible since guests had already paid for the meal.[10]

This peculiarly American system confounded and frustrated European visitors. Besides being rather rustic, it was confusing. In England, for example, a tavern was a tavern (it provided alcohol) and an inn was an inn (it provided lodging). Moreover, in cities like London and Paris there were many commercial venues to choose from when it came to mealtime; travelers did not necessarily have to dine at the inn where they were sleeping.[11] Even in French hotels, the traditional table d'hôte approach of requiring guests to pay for their board along with their room and then demanding that they show up to eat only at preestablished times was dying out by the early nineteenth century. This change was brought about as diners began to take advantage of the explosion in public restaurants the country was experiencing in the wake of the French Revolution, which eliminated guild laws that had once strictly limited the number of licensed food purveyors.[12]

In early-national America, however, local residents rarely ate anywhere besides their homes. The most favored taverns and hotels played host to civic and social banquets, but they were mostly for special occasions. Travelers too continued to have few dining options.[13] A category of business known as "victualler" catered primary to sailors.

A notable exception to the general system of tavern keeping in Boston was an establishment known as Julien's Restorator, a small hotel opened in 1793 on Congress Street and later moved to the corner of Milk and Congress. Operated by French refugee Jean Baptiste Gilbert Payplat dis Julien, or Mr. Julien, the "King of Soups," as he became known, Julien's meal service was modeled after the restaurants of his native Paris (*restorator* was an attempt to Anglicize the French word *restaurant*) that served á la carte meals at all times of the day.[14] Julien's was also similar to Parisian restaurants in that he marketed his fare as health food, serving rich broths and consommés meant to "restore" health. Julien advertised his hotel to wealthy merchants and developed a reputation for both the excellence of his French cookery and his wine cellar.[15]

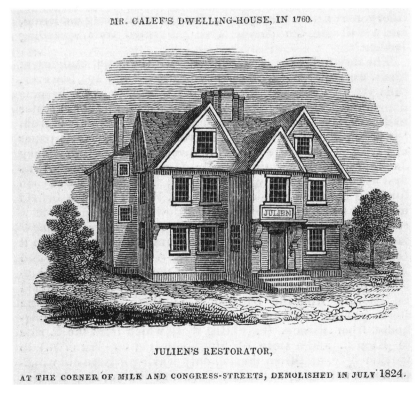

Exterior of Julien's Restorator, a hotel opened in 1793 and modeled on Parisian restorators. From Caleb Snow, *History of Boston* (1825).

Exterior of the Exchange Hotel, completed in 1809. From William Ukers, *All about Coffee* (1922).

In 1806, construction began in Boston on a new venture, the Exchange Hotel, also known as the Exchange Coffee House Hotel. The Exchange was one of the first buildings in America purposefully constructed to be a hotel. Improvements in transportation, combined with Boston's role as a hub of merchant activity and the beginnings of the factory system in the hinterlands, meant that the port town increasingly attracted travelers of substantial economic means.[16] Boston's existing (and confusing) assortment of inns, taverns, and hotels could no longer handle the growing number of visitors. The Exchange was mammoth for its day: nine stories high and containing three hundred guestrooms. Its striking neoclassical architecture further distinguished it from previous hotels. When the construction was finished in 1809, the Exchange was acknowledged to be the "most elegant hotel in the United States."[17] It soon gained a wealthy and fashionable patronage, even hosting President Monroe in 1817. Its dining arrangements, however, were essentially the same as in the city's older hotels; the dining room was simply larger. There were no real improvements in the level of quality or sophistication of the meals the Exchange offered, or in the way its dining room was used.

AMERICAN CULINARY AND CULTURAL ANXIETIES

As is evident in the descriptions of tavern and hotel fare above, American meals in the colonial and early-national periods were hearty but characterized primarily by their simplicity and straightforwardness. Originally forged in the demanding wilderness of the frontier, American appetites were the result of a complex process of cultural negotiation among the many different peoples who met each other in the New World. English culinary influences predominated, particularly among New Englanders. But even in New England, cookery tended to be plain when compared to English recipes, with simplified ingredient lists and cooking methods. New Englanders relied heavily on familiar foodstuffs they had known in England but incorporated native ingredients like corn and squash into their diets as well.[18]

America also obtained a reputation for having rather uncultivated—even vulgar—table manners. This reputation was due largely to the critical observations of opinionated European tourists. European travelers in America were generally affluent and accustomed to genteel behavior. During their stays in the States, they mostly observed Americans dining in the public context of the hotel or tavern, where, as we have seen, the table d'hôte approach encouraged diners to eat as fast as possible in order to get the most for their money. As a result, the high level of propriety practiced in many private American households did not exist in these settings. Indeed, one Englishman described the utter lack of decorum he observed at an American inn: "No ceremony was used. . . . Bones were picked with both hands; knives were drawn through the teeth with the edge to the lips. . . . Beefsteaks, apple tart, and fish were seen on the same plate the one moment, and had disappeared the next!"[19] European travelers were left to assume that the wolfish appetites they witnessed in these hotels were universally American.

Besides the speed with which Americans ate at hotels, the majority of European criticism centered on one core issue: the inadequate material culture of American dining settings. In England as in France, a fashionable meal required a vast array of physical objects, including an impressively sized dining table (or tables), sideboards, wall decorations, lighting devices, casters or cruets, decanters, fine cloths and napkins, scores of dishes, and individual table settings. The availability of such material luxury in America had certainly improved since the early eighteenth century. Most

Americans no longer dined "in common" from one communal bowl as many once had. But except in the very wealthiest of American homes, the assortment of dining equipment was still modest, particularly by elite European standards.[20] In most hotels, napkins and tablecloths were used multiple times between washings.[21] And as Margaret Hall explained to a friend back in England in the 1820s, "silver [four-tined] forks [were] a luxury not to be met with at the best inns in this country," which meant that Americans continued to use their "great lumbering, long, two-pronged forks," not to convey food to their mouths, as the English and French now did, but to assist them in cutting their meat.[22] Then, since the knife was already in their right hand, it was the knife that most Americans used to bring their bite of meat, and anything else on their plate, to their mouths. Hall observed: "It goes rather against one's feelings to see a prettily dressed, nice-looking woman ladling rice pudding into her mouth with the point of a great knife, and yesterday to my great horror I saw a nursery maid feeding an infant of seventeen months in the same way."[23] Numerous others confirmed Hall's observations about the provinciality of American dining settings and table manners.[24]

In the colonial period, barbs like Hall's would have deeply stung the pride of English-aping Americans. But in the years after the Revolution, America had endeavored to redeem its plain and practical fare and mode of eating as symbols of republican simplicity. For this, Europe's comparative culinary extravagance was a useful foil. According to Noah Webster in 1787, European civilizations were not unlike vegetables, "in their progress from their origin to maturity and decay."[25] The logic of this "conjectural theory of civilization" appealed to pundits in the early decades of American independence, jibing, as it did, with the republican political ideology that had set America on the path to revolution in the first place.[26] According to supporters of this theory, England had allowed itself to deteriorate into a nation divided between "Landlords, great noblemen and Gentlemen, extremely opulent, living in the Affluence and Magnificence" and a far greater majority who lived "in the most sordid wretchedness in dirty hovels of Mud and Straw," their spirits "tattered, dirty, and abject."[27] The result, according to Whig politicians, had been corruption and greed among the powerful few, who in their lust for yet more power and wealth had trampled on the liberties of their fellow countrymen in the American colonies. It was America's innocence and relative egalitarian conditions that had successfully allowed it to stand up to this corruption from abroad.

Now an independent America had the opportunity to start its civilization afresh. But only by eschewing aristocratic European models and avoiding the enervating influences of luxury would America avoid falling into the same downward spiral of historical decline as had Mother England. According to Webster, "It is perhaps always true that an old civilized nation cannot, with propriety, be the model for an infant nation, either in manners, fashions, in literature, or in government."[28] Such ideas encouraged Americans to take pride in their native customs and cuisine and avoid effeminate European displays of luxury. According to one good republican, the "well earn'd glory" of America would be "stuck to death with four-prong'd forks" or "brought to pass in knives of silver, and cut glass."[29] The beginning of the French Revolution, inspired by the principles of America's own, in 1789 held out some promise that France might now be regarded as a properly republican culinary model for America. Avowed Francophiles like Thomas Jefferson rejoiced. But the radical turn of France's revolution in 1793, combined with strong Federalist sentiments in New England, continued to make French influences problematic in Boston.[30]

In truth, however, Americans never fully rejected European cultural standards. The dilemma Americans found themselves in was twofold: how to balance republican simplicity against the need to cultivate national legitimacy and prestige, which required a certain level of pomp and elegance; and how to preserve social divisions and rank so that republicanism did not degenerate into mob rule.[31] People like Webster advocated for uniquely American standards of taste and erudition rather than those imported from abroad.[32] But who would decide what these American standards would be? In the meantime, Americans continued to compare themselves to European modes and felt self-conscious about Europeans' ridicule of their manners and food.

BOSTON BECOMES REFINED

In the late 1820s, Bostonians decided something must be done to elevate American foodways and, by extension, American culture and society. In the early nineteenth century, a strong feeling of national pride and purpose permeated the city, now a hub of commercial activity and an important financial center. Bostonians continued to strive to live up to the city's legacy as the "city upon the hill," reinterpreting that dictum to mean that Boston should help advance American civilization by becoming the paragon of cultural, educational, and humanitarian values.[33] These sentiments took on new urgency in the mid-1820s with the national decline of the Whig political party, centered in New England. The Boston elite was determined to spread its influence through culture if not politics.[34] Their efforts had tangible consequences; Boston developed into a powerhouse of literature, learning, and reform in the 1800s. If American foodways required a makeover, Bostonians believed their city was just the one to provide it.

By the early nineteenth century, the same prominent Boston families that had helped to usher in the market revolution by investing in new financial, transportation, and manufacturing enterprises were bemoaning the rapid social changes that resulted from it. Above all, they feared the breakdown of social stability and order by the unleashing of chaotic individualism. It was partly in an effort to combat this that leading Bostonians committed themselves to the ideals of social progress and personal perfectibility, consolidating their cultural power in civic and political institutions when national politics turned against them in 1828.[35] Classically republican ideas about the enervating and feminizing effects of luxury lingered, but elite Boston rehabilitated material prosperity as a symbol of achievement and necessary for generating a civilized society.[36] Prominent Bostonians also pursued refinement intended to further legitimize their own elevated positions in society and provide a model of socialization for others.

The ideology of refinement, as historian Richard Bushman has demonstrated, promulgated a hierarchy of merit, not birth.[37] Refinement offered the hope that anyone could become respectable simply by amassing certain key outward tokens of taste and gentility (like the proper kind of fork) and adopting refined modes of behavior. Such modes, Americans believed, could be acquired by anyone dedicated to learning them (an important reason for the deluge of etiquette guides published in this period) and thus did not interfere with democratic values. Moreover, according to the ideology of refinement, the knowledge and demonstration of genteel behavior were outward tokens of inner virtue.[38] In other words, Americans in this period saw refinement not as a product of privilege but as its cause. Knowing how to properly hold a four-tined fork and to use it to place food in one's mouth thus allowed diners to validate their elevated status and justify their claims to cultural influence.[39]

Ironically, the spread of refinement was made possible by the same democratic capitalism the effects of which it was supposed to mitigate. By the late 1820s, myriad new consumer goods made their way into American households thanks to a combination of innovative technology, better transportation, and the rise of American manufacturing.[40] Consumer items once reserved solely for the wealthiest members of society were now accessible to a broader range of the American public. These changes were especially evident in the realm of dining accoutrements. For example, after 1770, the handles of silver knives and forks, once made of solid metal and very expensive, could be fabricated from thin sheets of silver, machine stamped, and filled with resin or pumice. This method halved the cost of these items and became the standard process of production by 1820. Hand-powered stamping devices became power-driven after 1840, which, combined with the invention of electroplating around the same time, put a steadily expanding variety of tableware within the reach of ordinary Americans. Eventually, a mind-numbing array of increasingly specialized tableware—including bread knives, soup spoons, and sorbet spoons, as well as forks for fish, forks for shrimp, forks for salad, forks for terrapin, forks for lobster, forks for berries, and countless others—was also available.[41]

The lure of demonstrating respectability through the acquirement of these goods ensured mass demand for tableware, as well as for dining tables and chairs, candlesticks, and so on. But the consumer revolution hardly created a more equal society. Those without access to these goods were pushed further to the cultural margins. Moreover, as material life generally improved, those at the top of society turned to ever more elaborate and ostentatious displays of consumption to distinguish themselves from those below.[42] The decades after the Civil War witnessed the full fruition of the logic of using extravagant displays of wealth as the surest means to signal membership among the elite and the powerful; refinement provided the bridge that gradually enabled republican America to embrace such extravagance. In the meantime, refinement helped a generation of Americans stabilize social identity and order as they transitioned from a traditional world of entrenched social relationships to a rapidly changing and anonymous urban one.[43]

Dining rituals were significantly shaped by the ideology of refinement; they also served as refinement's greatest test. Comporting oneself properly while eating—using the correct fork and understanding how to hold it, wiping one's fingers on a napkin instead of one's own clothes or the tablecloth (or worse—licking them), chewing without giving offense to others at the table—all of this demanded access to key goods as well as specialized knowledge and skill about how to use them. Having found a way to successfully reconcile luxury and gentility with republicanism, Bostonians were eager to demonstrate their newfound gentility by sitting down to a meal. But they needed a new venue.

THE TREMONT HOUSE

In the late 1820s, the most refined settings for dining were private homes. Boston's public accommodations were all outdated—especially since the Exchange Hotel, previously the city's largest and most elegant, had burned to the ground in 1818.[44] A replacement was hastily constructed, but on a significantly more modest scale than the original. Given Boston's prestige as a hub of commerce and finance on the rise, the number of important businessmen and tourists traveling through the city, and the city's high cultural aspirations, Bostonians felt particularly self-conscious at having been left "without a hotel corresponding to the expectations and wants" of its most distinguished residents and visitors.[45] As one newspaper columnist lamented, Boston's existing "public houses of entertainment are hardly up to this purpose."[46] And so Bostonians began calling for a new venture.

William Harvard Eliot, a lawyer from a prominent Boston merchant family, spearheaded the planning and financing of the Tremont House Hotel (named for Boston's original designation as Trimountain). What Eliot had in mind for his hometown was not an ordinary hotel. He had no intention of building another traditional American inn, not even one so large as the original Exchange. Nor did he want to merely copy European hotels. Instead, he envisioned an entirely innovative and distinctively American public institution that would announce to the world the vibrancy of American civilization and provide a suitably appointed backdrop in which elites could demonstrate refinement and cement their

Conflagration of the Exchange Coffee House, by John Ritto Penniman (1824), shows the fire that destroyed the original Exchange Hotel. It was rebuilt less expensively after this fire and operated as a tavern until 1853. Private collection.

status and authority.[47] Eliot enlisted the talents of Isaiah Rogers, a pioneer of Greek revival architecture in Boston, who designed the building in the same monumental style as the State House and Quincy Market. Eliot then conscripted investments from 144 of Boston's most esteemed families and entrepreneurs in order to help finance the hotel's construction. Their investments were funneled through a company that the legislature of the Commonwealth of Massachusetts incorporated for just this purpose, under the understanding that, though privately owned, the hotel would serve the public interest. Thus from its very conception, the Tremont represented the partnership between civic and private purposes that Boston's leadership intended it would also facilitate.[48]

The total cost of constructing Eliot's dream hotel was $300,000, a staggering sum for the time. But when the Tremont opened in the fall of 1829, it was immediately recognized worldwide as something entirely new and different in the realm of innkeeping. Indeed, everything about the Tremont House—its contemporary neoclassical design, white Quincy granite exterior, 170 guestrooms (each with an individually keyed lock to protect guests' privacy, a new concept in innkeeping), innovative call-bell

The exterior view of the Tremont House Hotel, designed by Isaiah Rogers in 1829. Painting by James Bennett, circa 1830s.

system (allowing guests to summon a representative of the hotel from their rooms), indoor plumbing, and gas lighting—was modern and luxurious even by European standards.[49]

Upon opening, the hotel was put under the professional management of Dwight Boyden, a member of an old and respected Boston family.[50] Under Boyden's careful and innovative management, the hotel garnered superlatives from Americans and Europeans alike. In the 1830s, British diplomat Charles August Murray hailed the Tremont as "one of the proudest achievements of American genius," while his fellow Englishman James Boardman described it as "the largest and certainly the most elegant building of the kind in America."[51] Godfrey Vigne, globetrotter and English cricket player, praised the Tremont as "by far the best hotel in the United States." Even Charles Dickens called it "excellent" during his notorious 1842 tour of America, during which he was critical of almost everything else he experienced. And as late as 1852, a spread in the national magazine *Gleason's Pictorial* referred to the Tremont as "this most favorite house."[52] In addition to being admired, the Tremont was also immediately and widely copied throughout the nation. This imitation was something Eliot himself directly encouraged when he published a lavishly illustrated book, *A Description of the Tremont House,* in 1830. This book contained detailed descriptions and architectural drawings of the hotel intended to assist other cities in building their own versions.[53]

The centerpiece of Boston's magnificent new hotel, as everyone, including Eliot, readily acknowledged, was its main dining room. From here, the Tremont endeavored to transform American appetites, redefining American dining in several ways. Most important, it recast eating as an act of commercial, public consumption. As we have seen, prior to its opening, dining in a public setting had generally been reserved for traveling or special occasion civic banquets; Americans nearly always ate at home. But the Tremont changed this by accommodating both distinguished guests of the city as well as Boston's local residents.

Indeed, the hotel's developers envisioned the Tremont as a public extension of elite private dining rooms, a venue for regular business and civic association meetings and political fetes, as well as for private celebrations and general social networking. Meals were still included in the cost of rent for the hotel's lodgers, but for Boston's local residents there was now also the option to pay simply for a meal and the experience of dining out. The location of the hotel at the southwest corner of Beacon and Tremont (formerly Common) Streets, a neighborhood one guidebook referred to as the "Heart of the City," put the Tremont within the convenient reach of Boston's most esteemed residents.[54] Within just a few blocks were such important civic buildings as the Tremont Theatre (also designed by Rogers), the Congregationalist Park Street Church, and the golden-domed State House. The area also contained many upperclass homes. In fact, all of the original investors in the venture lived within a half-mile radius of it.[55]

In addition, the Tremont elevated the act of dining to a new height of luxury and refinement. No expense or effort was spared to make the experience of dining as opulent as possible. The Tremont cast aside classical republican concerns about the corrupting effects of luxury, applying instead modern understandings of material prosperity as an engine of progress and a symbol of civilization. In the dining room, Eliot took considerable care in creating a beautiful and lavish environment, seeing

This painting depicts Tremont Street, facing north. Beyond the Old Granary Burying Ground (at left) is the Tremont House Hotel (center). Across the street from it is Tremont Theatre, another Greek revival building also designed by architect Isaiah Rogers. Philip Harry, *Tremont Street, Boston*, circa 1843. Private collection.

"no impropriety in surrounding its occupants with tasteful and cheerful objects." As he explained, "As the largest and most public apartment of the house, [the dining room] was considered deserving of the most elaborate decoration."[56] Elaborate, indeed.

The main dining room spanned an area seventy-three feet long, thirty-one feet wide, and fifteen feet high. Fourteen ionic columns framed a sixty-by-twenty-foot space where long banquet dining tables were arranged in a U-shape around the perimeter. The ceiling was paneled, both so it would appear higher than it actually was and to provide better acoustics for guests' dinnertime conversations. The walls were also paneled. Turkish carpets covered the floor, and glass chandeliers hung from the ceiling. The furniture was ornately carved of dark walnut. Some of this furniture had been imported; the rest had been carved by the most

This map indicates the location of the Tremont House Hotel, opened in 1829.

skilled and respected New England craftsmen.[57] The room contained two open fireplaces, each capped with a marble mantle and decorated with French ormolu clocks. Six large, multipaned windows looked out onto busy Beacon Street, while French doors opened onto a piazza in the central courtyard. Additional light, intended not so much for practicality as to enhance the overall sense of theatricality in the room, flickered from gas lamps lining the walls.[58] The total effect succeeded in impressing patrons; the dining room was the most frequently described and admired aspect of the hotel.[59] The table settings provided at the Tremont were equally elaborate. White damask cloths and napkins, eye-catching flower arrangements, and an assortment of specialized glasses, plates, bowls, and flatware adorned the tables.

Interior of the main dining room at the Tremont House Hotel. From *Gleason's Pictorial* (1852).

The Tremont introduced an unprecedented level of ritual and drama to American dining. Patrons were not just eating at the Tremont: they were publicly declaring their personal refinement and testifying to America's progress as a civilized nation. Accordingly, every meal at the hotel was a performance. Meals continued to be served at prearranged times. Four a day were provided in the main dining room: breakfast at 7:30 a.m, dinner at 2:30 p.m., tea at 6 p.m., and supper at 9 p.m.[60] The midafternoon dinner was the largest meal served and always the best attended. Diners gathered outside of the main dining room in anticipation of the meal, which was announced by the clanging of a loud Chinese gong, one feature of the hotel that continued to be ridiculed by English visitors. Charles Dickens, for example, wrote, "The advent of each of these epochs [meals] in the day is proclaimed by an awful gong, which shakes the very window frames as it reverberates through the house, and horribly disturbs

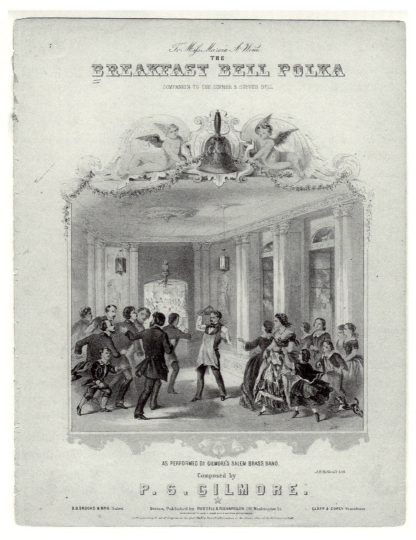

This image illustrates a feature of early-nineteenth-century American hotels that was routinely ridiculed by European tourists: the ringing of a bell or gong to signal the start of a meal. "The Breakfast Bell Polka," lithograph by J. H. Bufford, circa 1858. Library of Congress Prints and Photographs Division.

DINING AT THE TREMONT

Patrons at the Tremont no longer sat down to a groaning board already overburdened with the entire meal from soup to dessert, as at most other hotels in America. Nor did the guests serve themselves. Instead, the Tremont followed the considerably more elaborate and novel "French style" of service. French style was also known as *dining à la Russe* because it had been the Russian ambassador to France who in 1815 first introduced to Parisians the style of serving individual courses one at a time rather than blanketing the table with the entire meal and expecting guests to fill their own plates. Patrons chose individual dishes they would like to eat from a bill of fare (a new prop in the performance of refined dining), and waiters then carved, plated, and garnished the requested items as necessary, delivering them to each guest in single-size servings. This eliminated the chaotic frenzy of the table d'hôte to claim the best dishes. Guests still dined together at long banquet tables, taking their seats all at once as in more traditional meal settings. But the rest of the meal was clearly more segmented.

A large band of waiters was integral to the successful execution of the French style of service. Each waiter typically waited on three or four people.[62] All the waiters were men. Throughout the meal, the waiters were expected to cater to a diner's every demand, refill water and wine glasses, and bring anything they might desire from the kitchen. Besides providing service, waiters also contributed to the theatricality of the meal. Boyden, the first manager of the Tremont, introduced a kind of military drill for his waitstaff to perform at the beginning of dinner specifically for the purpose of adding drama: after a headwaiter gave a signal, the other waiters came marching out in formation to serve the guests. One Bostonian remembered:

> At the sound of a bell one [waiter] seized upon a quantity of plates, another knives, a third forks, a fourth a lot of large soup spoons, and a fifth the smaller spoons. At the second sound of the bell they moved into line, and at the third marched with sedate steps behind the chairs of the guests and

simultaneously the bearers of plates, knives, forks, and spoons, with a flourish of the hand, placed the different articles upon the table before the guest, and then gracefully stepped back into line ready to carry out their orders.[63]

This drill had the added benefit of helping to draw attention to the rich assortment of dining utensils provided at the Tremont.

Once the meal began, waiters were supposed to stand directly behind patrons as they ate, ready to hear and respond instantly to any request. But waiters rarely got to stand still for long. One patron explained how busy the diners kept the waiters, recalling that throughout the meal the waiters dashed "to and fro, amidst a running fire of champaigne corks."[64] Waiters cleared bowls, plates, glasses, and silverware as diners finished with them. They brushed down the table to remove crumbs before the dessert course.[65] The patrons' lavish consumption kept waiters very busy.

Diners navigated their way through the meal using the bill of fare, or menu.[66] This was basically a list of all the dishes the kitchen had available for each course. Such a list became necessary once offerings were no longer placed in plain sight on the table but were kept in the kitchen until a waiter retrieved them upon a patron's request. As one diner at the Tremont, picking up a bill of fare, explained to his friends: "I always run my eye over the list of dishes . . . and make up my mind which, and how many, of the good things I shall feed upon."[67] For about the first decade, Tremont bills of fare were handwritten by the manager or a member of the kitchen staff. Later, a local publisher began printing them on a single half-sheet of paper. An engraving of the exterior of the hotel adorned the top of the Tremont's menu, as if to remind patrons of the stately, public establishment in which they dined. The Tremont printed fresh menus each day, with the date inscribed at the top. The rest of the type was rarely reset. Bills of fare thus listed every possible concoction the kitchen might ever produce. Season and market restraints tended to go blissfully ignored, and instead the management might go through with a pencil and lightly check items to indicate which were actually available on a particular day. Some Tremont menus also included blank lines at the top on which to indicate that day's specials.[68]

The food was perhaps the most novel feature of the entire hotel. The Tremont introduced a heavily French-influenced menu and hired a classically trained French chef, Ferdinando Gori, to execute it.[69] Why French

TREMONT HOUSE.

CARTE DU DINER.

JUNE 16, 1843.

2 POTAGES.
Le Potage à la Tortue de mer,   Le Potage à la Reine.

7 RELEVES.
Le Saumon à la Mayonnaise,
Le Bass, sauce à la Hollandaise,
La Morue, sauce aux huitres,
Le Mouton, sauce aux capres,
Le Dindon, sauce aux huitres,
Le Jambon sur un socle à la moderne,
Les Chapons au cochon.

15 ENTRÉES.
Le Filet de boeuf piqué, garniture d'atelettes,
L'Aspic de homard sur un socle de cotelettes de veau en belle vue,
Les Ris de veau en paniers aux truffes,
L'Aspic d'huitres garni à la moderne,
Les Patés de gibier à la perigueux,
La Lunette de veau aux epinards,
L'Aspic de dindon sur un socle, garni d'atelettes,
La Paté chaude à la financière
La Croustade de pain garnie de gibier à l'Italienne,
Les Anguilles piqués à la sauce autrichienne fumée,
Les petits poulets aux truffes à la provençale,
Les Suprêmes de canard à la picaralda,
La Salade de homard à la garniture d'anguilles,
Les Filets de tortue sautés à la parisienne,
Le Pain de foie garni aux grenades de volaille.

5 HORS D'OEUVRES.
Le Jardinier de macaroni à l'Italienne,
Les Flans d'epinards garnis à l'écarlate,
Le Pain de foie, garniture de croutons,
Les petits pois à la parisienne,
Les Flans de pommes de terre à la chevalière.

12 ROTS.

Saddle of Mutton,	Brant,
Red-breasts,	Beetle-heads,
Yellow-legs,	Black-breasts,
Widgeon,	Green Geese,
Tame Ducks,	Turkies,
Wild Pigeons,	Chickens.

2 PIÈCES DE TABLE.
Les Monumens montés au sucre,
Les Corbeilles au nougat garnies aux oranges.

14 ENTREMETS.
La Charlotte Russe à la Parisienne,
La Crème fouettée au marasquin,

Le fromage à la Royale,	Gelée au Rhum,
Le Chantilly à l'Italienne,	Gelée aux fraises,
Les gateaux de Savoie,	Gelée au marasquin,
Paté aux pêches,	Paté à la rhubarbe,
Tarte aux groseilles,	Tarte aux pommes,
Poudins à la diplomate,	Poudins au nid d'oiseau.

FRUITS ET GLACES.

CAFÉ ET LIQUEUR.

Eastburn's Press—18 State Street.

Tremont House Bill of Fare dated June 16, 1843. Courtesy of American Antiquarian Society.

food? France had established itself worldwide as a culinary tour de force beginning in the Renaissance period, but Americans had long dismissed French food as foreign and pretentious.[70] Thomas Jefferson, for example, had garnered criticism for putting on airs when he returned from a trip to France in the 1780s with an appreciation for French cookery and a new willingness to "abjure his native victuals."[71] The association between French food (especially the haute cuisine of Paris) and conceit in America stemmed from two main sources: the origins of high French cuisine in the Parisian aristocracy, and the special training and skill required of French chefs. Professional cooks in France in this period endured years of formal, demanding apprenticeships before receiving the title *chef de cuisine*.[72] There was no such culinary training program yet in America where, as we have seen, cookery was considerably more straightforward.

Americans continued to disdain French food for its fussiness even as American interest in other aspects of French culture crested on the receipt of French assistance in the American Revolution and then with France's own revolution in 1789. For example, in 1793, Boston held a banquet dinner to celebrate the new French Republic. Attendees delighted in calling each other "citizen" and otherwise strove to demonstrate sympathy with the principles of *liberté* and *égalité*. But no French food was served. Instead, Bostonians killed a thousand-pound ox to honor the French revolutionaries, gilded its horns, and roasted its meat, which they served alongside bread and very strong punch on long tables that had been set up on State Street (formerly King Street).[73] While Americans celebrated the (early) French Revolution as gloriously republican, they still dismissed French cuisine as aristocratic.

By the early nineteenth century, little had changed in American attitudes toward French cuisine. The French refugee Julien, as mentioned earlier, attempted to Gallicize Boston's appetites at his hotel on Milk Street. Native Bostonians, however, remained mostly uninterested in Julien's complicated and expensive French cuisine.

But by the mid-1820s, there was evidence that Boston was beginning to amend its tastes to become at least slightly more amenable toward French cooking. When the Marquis de Lafayette, friend and hero of the American Revolution, visited the city in 1824, Boston feted him with a banquet at the (second) Exchange House. This banquet featured a prodigious selection of traditional Anglo-American dishes like "cod's head and shoulders" and boiled mutton. However, these American dishes were served alongside many French ones, including beef wrapped in pastry, crepes with jam, and blancmange.[74] The Exchange attempted to leverage the refinement and sophistication associated with French cuisine in order to elevate the overall status of the event itself. But in presenting honorific French fare alongside traditional American dishes, the Exchange also made a political statement about the equal value of American cookery.

The Tremont House adopted a similar approach with its menu. In addition to adopting the French style of serving dinner as a series of courses, the Tremont took full advantage of the honorific status of French food by hiring a French chef and embracing that cuisine. The hotel added yet another hint of erudition and prestige by describing the French dishes on its menu in French, not a language taught in American schools at this time. The ability to speak or read French was thus rare and signaled a worldly education.[75] These elements of dining *à la française* at the Tremont provided patrons a special opportunity to demonstrate their specialized knowledge and sophistication.

The Tremont's fare, however, was not entirely French. A close survey of the hotel's surviving menus reveals additional culinary influences, including Anglo-American, German, and Italian. Even the presumably French dishes these menus list are often more of a fusion between French and traditional American cooking, probably due to the abilities of the kitchen staff (not everyone employed had been trained in France as a chef) and the ingredients available.[76] Moreover, it is important to realize that American fascination with French cuisine had less to do with its being French per se—after all, French peasant food was not represented on the Tremont's menu—than it did with Americans' belief that the French were the world's culinary arbiters. Thus, when dishes like baked beans and pork appeared alongside others like *Fricandeu do veu, Sauce Tomate*—as they often did at the Tremont—the presence of French influences and language served to elevate the sophistication of the entire menu while suggesting that traditional American dishes were also among the de rigueur cuisines of the world.[77] The combination of influences further prevented the Tremont's menu from being perceived as too foreign or aristocratic—terms that still carried negative connotations in early nineteenth-century America.

Dinner at the hotel began with a selection of soups, including consommé, followed by a fish course. There were typically seven to ten different kinds of fish from which to choose, each with a different French sauce. Raw oysters were often among the selections, a delicacy New Englanders ate with great gusto. Following the fish were the entrées, side dishes served before the main course that showcased the full virtuosity of the chef. The Tremont usually offered at least fifteen different selections of entrées, including such dishes as *Ris de Veu,* or sweet breads; lobster presented in aspic; *les Patés de gibier à la perigeux,* or paté, of wild game with a sauce of *foi gras* and truffles; and *escallopes d'huitres.* After this course, the diners moved on to the roast meats and game. Then arrived the desserts, followed by a variety of fruits, coffee, and liqueurs.[78] Bordeaux, Rhine wines, Spanish wines, sherry, champagne, port, and, of course, Madeira (a longtime Boston favorite) were available to complement the meal. Guests could order as many dishes as they liked without incurring additional cost; only alcohol was extra.

The various elements of the Tremont dining experience elevated the act of eating to an entirely new kind of public consumption, one set in beautiful surroundings and organized around the enjoyment of good food. Boston responded enthusiastically. Young Bostonian Charles Wiggin declared that nowhere had he enjoyed a dinner that could rival one at the Tremont.[79] Irish writer and actor Tyrone Power pronounced the food at the Tremont the best he had tasted in America, and even the finicky Englishman William Charles MacReady observed that a meal he enjoyed there "might challenge the Trois Fréres" restaurant in Paris.[80]

Of course, the pleasures of dining at the Tremont came with a hefty price tag: lodgers at the hotel paid two to four dollars per day for room and board. The cost of dinner without lodging was one dollar (not including alcohol).[81] Along with being refined, dining at the Tremont was also expensive and, therefore, exclusive.

THE TREMONT AND ITS SUPPORTERS
RESPOND TO CHARGES OF ARISTOCRATIC PRETENSION

What about traditional republican admonishments to avoid imitation of European manners and culture? Was this not, some cultural critics charged, exactly what the Tremont had done: merely imported aristocratic European modes for Americans' (literal) consumption? What had happened to the calls earlier in the century to create distinctively American manners and fashions and cultivate native standards of taste? What about preserving egalitarianism as opposed to drawing attention to extremes of wealth? Would not the kind of luxury the Tremont put on public display be the death knell of the republic?

In the 1830s and 1840s, the answers to these questions varied depending on who answered them. There were those who continued to advocate for the development of uniquely American mannerisms and customs and who spoke out against the importation of European fashions. For example, Eliza Farrar maintained in her etiquette guide *The Young Lady's Friend* (1837) that Americans' use of the knife in feeding themselves was a matter of national identity that should not be cast off:

> If you wish to imitate the French or English, you will put every mouthful into your mouth with your fork; but if you think, as I do, that Americans have as good a right to their own fashions as the inhabitants of any other countries, you may choose the convenience of feeding yourself with your right hand, armed with a steel blade; and provided you do it neatly, and do not put in large mouthfuls, or close your lips tightly over the blade, you ought not to be considered as eating ungenteelly.[82]

But by this time, most other American-published etiquette guides disagreed with Mrs. Farrar and strove to stamp out the embarrassing habit of knife eating by encouraging Americans to become more like Europeans in their use of the fork.[83] These writers concluded it was better to adopt European mannerisms than for America to continue to be viewed as backward and uncouth.

The debate over the appropriateness of French cuisine was more divisive. Advocates for the appreciation of French cookery in America argued that there was nothing wrong with Americans enjoying French dishes and adopting French culinary techniques. From their point of view, Americans should be proud that in their country a cuisine originally developed for foreign aristocracy could be enjoyed by the masses.[84] And, as explained above, the Tremont's supporters could argue that since a few traditional American dishes appeared on the menu side by side with French ones, the hotel had not abandoned traditional American cookery but had elevated it to the same status as French cuisine. Still, the clear dominance of

French culinary influences in America's most elite restaurants—a trend that originated at the Tremont—continued to be controversial throughout the century.

Opinions about the level of luxury on display at the Tremont also differed sharply. In her housekeeping manual *The American Frugal Housewife* (1837), Lydia Marie Child warned her readers against the frivolities of new public amusements like the Tremont: "A luxurious and idle republic! Look at that phrase!—The words were never meant to be married together: everybody sees it would be the death of one of them."[85] Child pointed out a stark inconsistency between the displays of gentility and luxury that occurred at the Tremont and the democratic-republican values the hotel supposedly fostered: gentility's degradation of work. In its purest form, refinement imagined an existence free from work, an existence devoted purely to the pursuit of beauty and pleasure. Moreover, the attainment of refinement required heavy consumption, the antithesis of productive work. In these ways, refinement contradicted the spirit of republican government.[86] The Tremont's manager, developers, and patrons, however, denied this. They maintained that the hotel encouraged liberty and equality and promoted hard work of all kinds.

How did defenders of the Tremont support their claims? First of all, they pointed out that from its very inception the hotel was intended, as one historian has put it, "to symbolize the relationship in America between a free citizenry and free enterprise."[87] The hotel's supporters—most of them members of the Whig political party and champions of government-sponsored economic development—argued that the Tremont attracted commerce to Boston, thus generating widespread opportunity throughout the city and the country.[88] Moreover, in providing a stage for the enactment of refinement, its advocates argued that the hotel provided a model of success to which their fellow Bostonians could aspire. As Benjamin Franklin had put it, "Is not the Hope of one day being able to purchase Luxuries a great Spur to Labour and Industry?"[89] Such aspiration would be to the benefit first of individuals and then of the entire nation. Moreover, in comparison to institutions of the actual European aristocracy including restaurants, there were no overt barriers to enjoying the pleasures of a meal at the Tremont. All were welcome, as long as they could pay. For these reasons, the Tremont and other new hotels like it became known to their admirers as "palaces of the public."[90]

The Tremont also went out of its way to show that the hotel and the culture it promoted glorified labor, including manual labor. This was most clearly evident in the speeches given during the hotel's opening banquet praising the hard work of the tradesmen who had helped to construct the building. In addition to such speeches at the opening celebration, the hotel hosted a second banquet the next night specifically to pay tribute to the tradesmen. The Tremont invited 130 mechanics (mostly members of the Massachusetts Charitable Mechanics Association) to dine in its main dining room, likely the only time men of this economic class would ever eat at the hotel (because they did not have to pay for it). Mayor Josiah Quincy once again presided over the affair and Daniel Webster served as toastmaster. Several times over the course of the meal, the attendees raised a glass to the "mighty power of Mechanics," affirming the dignity of their work.[91] Clearly, the separate, class-segregated nature of these two dinners undermined the principles of social cohesion its supporters claimed the Tremont represented. Nevertheless, Boston's newspapers faithfully reported the testimonies given at each banquet that heralded the hotel as a monument to work, enterprise, and opportunity for all.[92]

The treatment of restaurant employees at the Tremont and the other elite dining venues that soon opened in imitation of it provides yet another window into these tensions. The luxury dining experience depended on an underclass of unskilled male laborers. (Women were eligible to work in other parts of the hotel as laundresses and maids, but not in the kitchen or dining room.) The only skilled job related to the dining room was that of the head chef, who was required to possess some kind of specialized culinary training. America continued to lack professional culinary education until late in the nineteenth century, and so most early chef jobs went to European immigrants who held (or at least claimed to hold) the preferred qualifications.[93]

Meanwhile, native-born white men scorned the remaining jobs as cooks and waiters because they considered them too servile for republican citizens to perform without losing a measure of their treasured independence. These jobs instead went to the dregs of Boston society, those whose occupational options were strictly limited due to racial and ethnic discrimination and prejudice against them: African Americans and Irish immigrants. Indeed, 59 percent of Boston's cooks, according to the 1850 federal census, were either nonwhite or foreign born. Of the waiters, 62 percent were nonwhite or foreign born.[94] This striking ethnic and racial composition of the workforce of Boston's restaurants did not go unnoticed by patrons. For example, when Englishman Sir John Acton visited the city in 1853, he remarked to his journal that Boston's waiters were overwhelmingly black or Irish men.[95] It is impossible to determine the kinds of venues in which those listed as "cook" or "waiter" in the census worked, but numerous travelers' accounts confirm that waiters in even the most elite venues in Boston were overwhelmingly black or Irish.[96]

The job of cook, in particular, was a hot, dirty, and generally thankless one, especially when compared to that of restaurant chef. Chefs in the 1800s—not unlike today—took most of the credit for the food produced in their kitchens, though their staffs performed much of the work. While chefs wore special uniforms signaling their professional status, no evidence suggests the rest of the kitchen staff did. Instead, cooks stood for long hours in front of burning hot stoves and ovens wearing their regular, food-splattered clothes. Luxury hotel kitchens like the Tremont's were typically located in basements below the dining rooms.[97] Waiters either went down to fetch patrons' food orders or called the orders out to members of the kitchen staff, who then hoisted servings up to the dining room in dumbwaiters to be delivered. As a result, cooks were invisible to the wealthy patrons for whom they cooked.

While chefs (especially French ones) often commanded outrageous salaries, especially later in the century, cooks possessed little bargaining power to achieve better pay or working conditions, especially in a city overflowing with recent immigrants in search of employment.[98] Wage figures for Boston's early-nineteenth-century restaurant cooks are not available, but in 1885 the *Boston Daily Globe* reported that the city's commercial cooks "did a man's work for pay that a tow-boy on a railroad would look at with scorn."[99] This observation is confirmed by the 1850 federal census, which reported that 82 percent of cooks lived with nonfamily members and a negligible number owned property. With such low status, poor working conditions, and low pay, it is no surprise that turnover among cooks was high.[100]

The Tremont's waiters could not be hidden away from public view like cooks. As we have seen, waiters were integral to the overall theatricality and enjoyment of a patron's fine dining experience. The Tremont's management accordingly decided it would be best for the democratic republican image of the hotel if waiters were promoted as respectable men doing a valuable job rather than as servile and therefore degraded

A black waiter, as depicted in William Dean Howell's *Their Wedding Journey* (1881).

workers. The Tremont's waiters did not wear livery, as waiters in Europe did, because of the association of livery with servitude. Throughout the first half of the century waiters instead wore dark shirts and pants, covered by a crisp white apron.[101] Management also initially prohibited patrons from tipping, or "feeing" the waiters, another European custom that Americans scorned. Management assured patrons that their waiters (unlike waiters in Europe) received adequate wages and that giving them "bonuses" was humiliating to the dignity of their labor.[102] Even the title *waiter* originated from an American desire to separate and elevate the work from serving. For example, in Royall Tyler's 1787 play *The Contrast*, Colonel Manly's servant explains that he prefers to be called a "waiter" because "no man shall master me!" In all these ways, the Tremont endeavored to present waiters as dignified laborers.[103]

Moreover, although there was no formalized instruction program for waiters, managers at elite venues like the Tremont realized that executing perfect table service required considerable practice and skill. Significant effort was thus expended in preparing the waiters to perform their jobs well. One guidebook published in 1848 by Tunis Campbell, an African American man and former Boston headwaiter, gave advice to hotel managers about how best to train waiters: "Waiting-men should be drilled every day except Saturday and Sunday."[104] Managers quickly learned to value good waiters and provided opportunities for promotion and wage increases to reward and retain the best ones. Waiters on staff at the Tremont, for example, were ranked, and those with greater abilities were given higher status and more esteemed tasks. Headwaiters also received more pay. The average wage for waiters in elite venues by the 1850s was between ten to sixteen dollars per month, making waitering one of the better-compensated nonskilled occupations in urban America.[105] Finally, in contrast to many other menial jobs, waitering provided steady, nonseasonal work that was not especially dangerous. Though native-born white Americans continued to avoid waitering if possible, for Irish immigrants and black men it was one of the best jobs available.

It is thus apparent from this brief comparison between chefs, cooks, and waiters that the elite Boston public was willing to ignore the servility and degradation of the employees with whom it did not interact. But with management's assistance, Bostonians endeavored to conform their treatment and view of the waiters who directly served them so as to

Portrait of Tunis Galic Campbell, a former Boston waiter, who published *Hotel Keepers, Head Waiters, and Housekeepers' Guide* in 1848, which proscribed very specific and demanding training for waiters.

better fit the ideal of the venue as a site promoting democratic republicanism as opposed to fostering aristocratic class distinctions.

The potential radicalism of this (admittedly contradictory) position was realized in the story of Shadrach Minkins. A fugitive slave from Norfolk, Virginia, Minkins had escaped to Boston in 1850 and taken a job as a restaurant waiter.[106] His arrival coincided with the passage of the

HOTEL KEEPERS,

HEAD WAITERS,

AND

HOUSEKEEPERS' GUIDE.

BY TUNIS G. CAMPBELL.

~~~~~~~

BOSTON:
PRINTED BY COOLIDGE AND WILEY,
12 WATER STREET.
1848.

Title page of *Hotel Keepers, Head Waiters, and Housekeepers' Guide* (1848).

second Fugitive Slave Act, and at the time Boston was on high alert for slave catchers. Unfortunately for Minkins, a "stout copper-colored man," two slave catchers arrested him as a fugitive at his place of work one Thursday morning in February 1851. They escorted Minkins to the court-house, where Boston authorities had no choice but to acquiesce in his removal back to the South.[107] But as word of the black waiter's arrest spread throughout the city, critics of slavery galvanized support for Minkins and for the antislavery cause through strongly worded newspa-per editorials that built on the (albeit limited) esteem that Boston afforded its waiters. Minkins was repeatedly depicted in these accounts as a trained, dedicated worker who had won the respect and admiration of his em-ployer and his customers. The writers emphasized that upon his arrest Minkins had been forcibly carried off from his workplace—still clad in his waiter's apron—where he had been endeavoring to earn an honest living. Such portrayals (combined with outrage of the Fugitive Slave Act) so infuriated Bostonians that before Minkins could be sent back south, an interracial mob stormed the courthouse where he was being held and dramatically carried him off. Unnamed individuals later hid Minkins and helped him to escape to freedom in Canada.[108]

From the historian's perspective, determining whether the Tremont had succumbed to imitation of aristocratic European culture or whether it lived up to the distinctively American values its defenders claimed for it is no less complicated than it was for contemporaries. Clearly, there was at least some mimicry going on. Lacking an established high culture of its own, affluent Bostonians transferred the culture of the European gentry to America, where they used it to justify their wealth and secure their political authority and social prominence. But they also used it to promote the American nation in the eyes of the world and to stimulate national economic growth. They saw refinement as an incentive that would help secure the expansion of free enterprise and promote the vir-tues of hard work and industry throughout the land. This was a compli-cated dynamic. As another historian, Richard Bushman, has so elegantly come to describe Americans' embrace of European culture, "the word is emulation, not imitation. The impulse was not to copy, but to partake— of power and of the glory, strength, and beauty" of those who had cre-ated these standards.[109] Just as surely as they adopted European cultural modes, Americans also adapted these modes for their own purposes.

RECONCILING EFFEMINATE LUXURY AND MASCULINITY

All this is not to say, however, that the Tremont's male patrons felt no discomfort in surrounding themselves with what might be seen as effeminate luxury. All protestations to the contrary aside, there was in fact a profound tension between the hotel's opulence and its intended civic and commercial purposes. The hotel's management actively strove to resolve this tension in a number of ways. First and foremost, women were initially excluded from the main dining room. The Tremont instead provided a separate dining space for women, which we will examine in another chapter. Men could thus feel more secure in their masculinity while indulging their tastes for luxury and refinement, which carried connotations of feminization and weakness.

Men's own behavior in the dining room also helped to define this space as properly masculine. From the day the Tremont opened, Bostonians used its dining room to host important political and economic functions, thus incorporating the hotel firmly within the male-gendered sphere of government and work.[110] Men also met at the Tremont at midday to conduct business over dinner.[111] The heavy drinking and cigar smoking—behaviors in which no respectable woman would have engaged—that took place around the hotel's banquet tables further secured the masculinity of the space. It may be that the speed with which diners ate was yet another deliberate attempt to assert masculinity in the face of the feminizing social controls imposed on men by the ideology of refinement and by the luxurious and therefore effeminate dining settings. European travelers in particular remarked on the haste with which Tremont diners consumed their meals. Englishman James Boardman observed: "The dispatch at meals, particularly among the mercantile classes, is almost incredible to those who have not witnessed it."[112] Boardman lamented that he "could not keep pace at meals with the Americans." Henry Tudor, while quite complimentary overall of the Tremont, similarly noted that its patrons ate extraordinarily quickly, especially at dinner. He attributed this habit to the "economizing diligence of the American people."[113] Rather than prolong the meal unnecessarily, relaxing over the table and continuing to enjoy the beautiful surroundings in which they found themselves—as women might—Boston men preferred to get back to work. This also exemplified yet another way in which the hotel promoted commerce. In all these ways, the Tremont's patrons strove to assert their

THE PARKER HOUSE AND
THE SHIFTING GOAL OF REFINEMENT

The success of the Tremont House quickly inspired a wave of imitators in Boston and in cities throughout the country.[115] In Boston, the Tremont's competitors soon included the American House, opened in 1835 on Hanover Street, and the Revere House, opened on Bowdoin Square in 1847. Both of these venues were built on essentially the same model as the Tremont, but each one tried to outdo the last in terms of the magnitude of its opulence and splendor, especially in the dining room. The attainment of refinement proved to be a shifting goal, as Bostonians eagerly sought out the most fashionable new dining venues.[116] Throughout the 1860s, these remained closely tied to first-class, incorporated hotels, probably due to the expense associated with erecting and operating such a business. There were exceptions, however—the most famous nationally being Delmonico's in New York.[117]

In 1832, Harvey Parker launched a freestanding, à la carte restaurant on Court Street in Boston. Parker named his venture the Tremont Restaurant in an effort to take advantage of the renown and the sense of local pride felt for the Boston hotel. Parker's restaurant, a single room located in a small cellar, lacked the physical splendor and stateliness of the original Tremont House. But Parker made up for this by providing his patrons the convenience of being able to dine whenever they chose, serving meals at all hours of the day.[118] Parker gradually attracted the attention of some of Boston's gourmands for his excellent quality fare. A letter to the *Boston Courier* in 1843 rhapsodized, "Salmon, turtle soup, &c., are to be found there in perfection, while the oysters—oh! Ye depopulated beds at Prince's Bay, how do ye rue the hour when Parker first determined to add your shelly treasures to his already abundant and luxurious carte."[119] Parker later became known for his lighter-than-air rolls.

In 1856, Parker capitalized on the success of his small restaurant and with a business partner opened his own magnificent five-story marble-covered luxury hotel on School Street.[120] The Parker House and Restaurant was the first in America to be conducted on the "European Plan," meaning that the costs of lodging and boarding were now separate.

The exterior of the Parker House Hotel, as seen from City Hall in 1856. From James W. Spring, *Boston and the Parker House: A Chronicle of Those Who Have Lived on That Historic Spot Where the New Parker House Now Stands in Boston* (Boston: J. R. Whipple, 1927).

Guests of the Parker House were welcome to dine in the hotel's outstanding French restaurant, as were local residents, or they could explore the city and try different venues. After all, Boston now enjoyed several superb public dining options, and visitors were eager to discover and compare the best places. Parker's Restaurant also continued to serve meals à la carte at all times.[121] These changes provided far greater flexibility and convenience and reflected the changing dining needs of a busy urban population.

The experience of dining at the Parker House was considerably less communal and more segmented than at the Tremont. Patrons no longer sat down together at one time, nor did they gather together around long banquet tables. Parker instead installed numerous smaller tables throughout his opulently decorated dining room that accommodated individual parties of guests. This transition extended guests greater privacy and encouraged them to come and go as they pleased. Besides being more

The Empty Dining-Room

This illustration from an 1899 edition of *Their Wedding Journey* by William Dean Howells depicts a well-appointed nineteenth-century hotel dining room with smaller tables to accommodate separate parties of guests. Note the African American waiters positioned behind each table, ready to cater to patrons.

convenient, this change also signaled that diners had become fully comfortable with the individual display of luxury.

Indeed, the second half of the century witnessed the complete embrace of what sociologist Thorstein Veblen called *conspicuous consumption* in America.[122] Urbanization, immigration, industrialization, and incorporation continued unabated, expanding the economy and making increasingly extravagant displays of wealth possible. Affluent Americans—the nouveau riche and the more established wealthy alike—persisted in their search for opportunities to publicly declare and legitimize their elite status and solidify their nation's claims to being a world power. The refined restaurant fit the bill perfectly.[123]

As restaurants became increasingly elaborate in the dining environments they offered and the foods they served, they became less concerned about charges of fostering aristocratic pretension or with modeling themselves after Europe. In fact, the very word *culture,* as historian Lawrence Levine has observed, was increasingly becoming synonymous with *European*.[124] Consequently, French cuisine was not just esteemed; it was consecrated. The formerly polyglot nature of upper-class restaurant menus disappeared, and restaurants in Boston and across the country thoroughly Gallicized their bills of fare to appeal to a public that now considered French cuisine the sine qua non of high culture.[125]

Tipping, a European custom that American restaurants had long eschewed, also began to be in vogue late in the century as a means to demonstrate the conspicuous consumption of waiters' service. Indeed, a steady stream of quarters (or more) ensured wealthy diners scores of fringe benefits courtesy of their satisfied waiter. An article in the *Boston Daily Advertiser* in 1888 explained how this dynamic worked in one of the city's most opulent (though unspecified) hotel dining rooms. According to the reporter, a man, whom the reporter referred to simply as "Moneybags," and his wife entered the hotel's dining room and were greeted by its headwaiter. The man then placed twenty-five dollars in the headwaiter's palm and pointed to the table at which he wished to be seated. Though the table was already occupied, the reporter watched as the waiter coolly walked over to its current inhabitants and informed them he would have to reseat them elsewhere. The reporter went on: "After being seated, Moneybags would send $25 to the head cook and he would send better prepared dainties. . . . Of course, one of the best waiters in the room would be detailed to wait on Moneybags and his wife and he, too, must be liberally fee'd."[126] Though this was an extreme example, countless additional newspaper stories in the late nineteenth century confirmed that tipping secured such advantages at restaurants as extraordinarily friendly greetings, expedited service, and even superior quality food.

A Parker House waiter interviewed in 1884 by the *Boston Daily Globe* reported that a couple from "one of the suburban towns" who dined at Parker's every Saturday evening tipped him, as their regular waiter, at least "half a dollar and often more." The waiter went on to say that while some customers offered tips only at Christmas, "the 'regulars' generally pay their waiters anywhere from $1 to $3 a week."[127] This comment underscores that those who could afford to eat out regularly could also most afford to tip.

The practice of tipping put refined dining even further beyond the reach of ordinary Bostonians. Patrons who could barely afford the fare at refined restaurants had even more difficulty coming up with extra quarters—let alone twenty-five dollars—with which to tip their waiter. Diners who could not afford to tip complained that as a result they not only missed out on the special advantages that tipping secured in elite restaurants but also suffered discrimination for failing to offer a tip. As the *Boston Daily Advertiser* surmised, "the customer who neglects to give a bonus to the waiter who serves him may be well served once, but never again."[128] For the affluent, using tips to make demands of—and receive favors from—waiters demonstrated that they belonged among the patriarchal classes of Europe. But for others, the practice of tipping put them at a distinct disadvantage within the milieu of the elite restaurant.

The demonstration of carefully cultivated social graces that dining in these restaurants demanded continued to help naturalize the extremes of wealth visible within them. The demonstration began with one's appearance; obvious care was taken by diners to dress finely and fashionably. Indeed, magazines and etiquette manuals began offering specific advice on how to dress for dinner at a hotel.[129] The demonstration continued with the dedicated and disciplined exhibition of bodily control and table manners throughout the entire meal. Even the act of sitting down to the table required poise. "Be seated with ease," one etiquette manual instructed, "without rattling your chair; not so far from the table as to endanger your dress in taking food or drink, nor so near as to press against the table and shake it at every movement of your body."[130] Failure to observe these rules of etiquette could be deeply humiliating. As one authority cautioned by 1872, "You are liable, at a hotel, . . . to be placed in a position in which ignorance of dinner etiquette will be very mortifying."[131] Ordering from the bill of fare was yet another test of one's sophistication. Selecting items in combination with one another to form a coherent, harmonious whole meal and pairing each course with its most complementary wine became matters of great pride and skill—and potential embarrassment. One authority explained in 1837: "To order a dinner well is a matter of invention and combination. It involves novelty, simplicity, and taste."[132] The challenge was certainly heightened when the menu was full of exotic French dishes and also partly written in French. Ordering in front of one's peers using the correct pronunciation of these French dishes added yet another hurdle. Thus the potential stumbling blocks of luxury restaurant dining were many, but the pay-off for successfully navigating through a meal was great: public validation of one's status and contribution toward a model of national progress and civilization.

In theory, elite venues supposedly remained "palaces of the public." However, Charles Wiggin's experience at Parker's in 1859 is revealing of just how discomforting dining in one of the city's refined venues could be to Bostonians who lacked sophisticated knowledge of refined behavior or French cookery (or both) or a sufficiently large pocketbook. Wiggin was a middle-class teenager who traveled frequently and loved good food. He had been longing to visit Parker's ever since it opened. Finally, one Thursday in July, he and another young friend decided to try it out. They entered the restaurant "with bold steps" and were shown to one of Parker's many tables. As they perused the French bill of fare, the boys found, to their great dismay, that beefsteak and fried potatoes were not listed. Not to be deterred, Wiggin asked their waiter whether beefsteak could be obtained and for how much. He noted in his diary that at this point the waiter "troubled us much" by leaning on the table, staring at the boys impatiently. The waiter replied that, yes, beefsteak could be prepared at a cost of forty cents. Potatoes would be an additional cost. In fact, as Wiggin observed, nothing on the menu at Parker's was less than thirty cents. Concluding that they could not afford to dine after all (forty cents was "far beyond our means"), and to make their escape with as little humiliation as possible, the boys told the waiter that they would need more time to make up their minds before they ordered. Then at the first opportunity they snuck out of the restaurant, "glad to get away." The boys made up their minds never to go to Parker's again unless someone else was to foot the bill.[133] For Wiggin and the vast majority of Bostonians, dinner at one of the city's refined venues was just too dear; Wiggin admitted that his own father called the prices at Parker's "absurd."[134] Luckily, there was now a wide variety of public dining establishments to cater to these Bostonians' more modest appetites.

The Tremont Hotel tried to keep pace with the constantly shifting and rising standards of luxury. It was remodeled in 1852 and placed under new management. Nevertheless, the hotel gradually fell into a "genteel decay," its dining room growing shabby and outmoded in comparison to its newer and more ornate competitors. A visitor in 1857 found the food and service still good, but the halls "empty and cavernous."[135] Times and tastes had changed. Ironically, the embrace of luxury the Tremont had initially capitalized on and helped to facilitate led to the hotel's own eventual eclipse as a cultural icon. It finally closed in 1894 and the building was razed in January 1895.

CHAPTER 2

Bolted Beef
and Bolted Pudding

Eating Houses

In June 1832, the Journeymen Ship Carpenters and Caulkers of Boston demanded a ten-hour workday that stretched from five a.m. to seven p.m. but included "an hour for breakfast, two hours for dinner, and half an hour for refreshments."[1] These men's concern over the amount of time their employers allowed for meals, especially dinner, reflected the recent assault of the emerging urban market economy on male workers' eating patterns. The midday dinner, a legacy of agricultural work rhythms, had traditionally been the largest, most significant meal of the day in America.[2] By the early 1830s, however, the time allotted for dinner had shrunk considerably. Some employees were given no break for their meal; others received well under an hour. Even self-employed men, who had more control over their work schedules, began to demonstrate what some considered an "excessive devotion to business" that made them loathe to leave their counting houses or offices for too long in the middle of the workday to dine.[3] These new time constraints on men's mealtimes had significant consequences for their appetites. First and foremost, men employed at any distance from their homes often found their schedules did not permit them to return there to eat. The eating house became a solution to this dilemma.

Men's commercial options for obtaining their midday meals grew and evolved throughout the century. Besides restaurants, there were the street vendors that had hawked oysters, roasted corn, sweets, and other foods to Bostonians of all classes since the colonial period. But beginning in the late 1820s a new kind of business increasingly began to address men's noontime appetites.[4] Eating houses, open from late morning to late afternoon, specialized in dinner and quickly became the most prevalent type of eatery in nineteenth-century Boston. These establishments provided a counterpoint to the city's luxury restaurants by offering straightforward, affordable, and, above all, fast midday meals intended to satisfy hungry men in a hurry. A broad range of men—including craftsmen like those of the Journeymen Ship Carpenters and Caulkers of Boston, factory and dockworkers, bankers, merchants, and professionals—all increasingly sought to purchase their dinners, sharing the experience of buying and eating food away from home.

The eating house trade was thus inspired by dramatic changes that occurred within American society and culture in the nineteenth century. The boundless growth of the market and consumption and the loosening of domestic ties altered how urbanites ate and gave rise to new habits and behaviors. The increasing segmentation and hierarchy of Boston society during this period was also reflected in the city's eating houses, with certain venues endeavoring to distinguish themselves in order to attract a more affluent clientele. And yet, although they were clearly divided along socioeconomic, racial, and ethnic lines, overall the city's eating houses helped in the creation of a more market-driven society and culture. They also contributed to the construction of broad new notions of urban masculinity by emphasizing emerging male-gendered traits like efficiency and economic productivity and by excluding women. As they fed men day after day, the city's eating houses facilitated Bostonians in bridging the transition between traditional and modern patterns of living, working, and manhood.

MASCULINE BASTIONS

Except for the occasional female proprietor, the nineteenth-century eating house was a masculine bastion.[5] For the first half of the century, women's employment options did not lead them to seek a rushed dinner in a downtown eatery as men's occupations increasingly did. The number of women employed in this period grew, but the most typical type of job for women was domestic service, which entailed taking meals in the homes of their employers.[6] Women doing outwork in their homes while tending to children and housework, another common source of income for antebellum Boston women, could eat their dinners at home.

As we will see in the next chapter, the expanding shopping duties and reform activities of more affluent, nonemployed women led them to seek commercial meals in the antebellum years, but they were not welcome in most eating houses (nor would they have wanted to dine there); they instead sought more leisurely and refined meals in establishments earmarked especially for them.[7]

The Eating House Genre

Hungry men in Boston knew where to go to find an eating house. Eating houses were densely clustered in the commercial heart of the city, which extended from the narrow strip of piers at the tip of the peninsula west of the waterfront to Washington Street, and from Water Street north to Ann Street.[8] Here, in close proximity to the majority of the city's

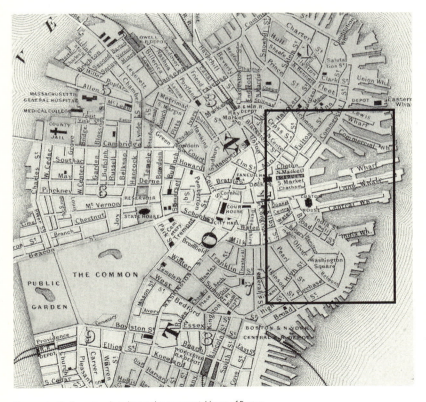

The area inside the rectangle indicates the commercial heart of Boston.

docks and factories, stores and counting houses, offices and workshops, men found it most convenient to purchase and eat their dinners. Later in the century, pockets of eating houses also emerged in South and East Boston, close to the newer factories that developed in these regions as they became more industrialized.

There was very little regulation of eating houses in Boston, and new ones opened all the time. Start-up capital was minimal. Proprietors were supposed to secure a license from the city, which required a fee, but there were undoubtedly many who did not bother. Penalties for operating without a license were only in place for those who sold alcohol in addition to food, and even then the rather stiff penalty, a $100 fine, was rarely enforced.[9] Nearly all proprietors ran their businesses from their homes, often enlisting the assistance of family members.[10] The domestic nature of such eating house businesses was a bit ironic since it was the increasing separation of work and home that made the trend toward dining in such a venue popular in the first place.

While getting into business was relatively easy, staying in business was another matter. Historian Richard Pillsbury has estimated that only 2 percent of the restaurants operating in 1850 were still in business ten years later.[11] The quickly proliferating nature of the eating house business meant that competition between eateries was especially stiff. Most eateries operated on very tight profit margins and did not have money to invest in marketing or frills. Few of Boston's eating houses had names more creative than their owner's or bothered with elaborate signage to announce their venue. Instead, one simple technique used to attract the attention of passersby was to attach bills of fare to string hung in the doorway, flapping in the wind. Other proprietors affixed chalkboards to their door on which they scrawled the day's menu items, hoping to entice customers inside.[12]

Boston's eating houses fed large, hungry crowds for low prices and in record time; a well-run venue could feed a man in less than ten minutes. Their busiest hours tended to be between eleven and three.[13] Patrons came directly from their workplaces, hungry for their midday meals. Since bills of fare were costly to print and required time to distribute, many proprietors dispensed with them and simply called out available dishes to patrons as they entered. Once they received their food orders, patrons ate as quickly as possible, taking only a short pause, according

560

Know all Men by these Presents,

That we *John Sanders, Nathan Randall & Samuel Chiswell*

all of the City of Boston,

are held and firmly bound unto the City of Boston, in the full and just sum of

Two hundred Dollars, to be paid to the said City or

its assigns; to which payment well and truly to be made, we bind ourselves

and every of us, our heirs, executors, and administrators, jointly and sever-

ally, firmly by these presents. Sealed with our seals. Dated this

Fifth day of *October* in the year of our Lord One

Thousand Eight Hundred and Twenty *nine*.

The Condition of this Obligation is such, That whereas the

above bounden *John Sanders* has been

duly licensed according to law, by the Mayor and Aldermen of said City

of Boston, as a *Victualler* at his House, Shop, or

Store, Number *Front* Street,

in said City, and at no other place, until the first day of July next, unless

sooner revoked or suspended by said Mayor and Aldermen. NOW IF

THE SAID *J Sanders* shall well and truly comply with

the terms of his said License, and all Laws and Regulations respecting such

licensed houses, then this Obligation is to be void; otherwise to remain in

full force, power and virtue.

Signed, sealed, and delivered
in presence of

George Clark

J. S.

John Sanders

Nathan Randal

Samuel Chiswell

A victualling license issued by the City of Boston. By 1829, this type of license permitted the holder to sell alcohol in addition to food (to be consumed on the premises). The State of Massachusetts prohibited operation of public bars throughout the nineteenth century, so victuallers and innkeepers were the only licensed purveyors of alcohol intended to be consumed on the premises. From the collections of the Boston City Archives.

to one source, "between bolted beef and bolted pudding."[14] The meal was typically washed down with cups of hot coffee, or, in those venues that sold alcohol, ale or whiskey.

Eating house proprietors and customers alike dispensed with propriety. In fact, this became one of the main attractions of the eating house, where convenience and speed reigned. The most important objective was simply to fill one's belly and get on with the workday. Customers typically did not squander precious time or effort making conversation with their fellow diners but focused instead on the main task at hand: eating. Indeed, first-time visitors to the eating house—especially critical English tourists—often expressed shock at the utter lack of sociability inside the typical American establishment.[15] When conversation did happen, it was made with mouths full of food, hands gesticulating between bites. All pretense of decorum was abandoned. As one Boston newspaper explained later in the century, tongue in cheek, eating house etiquette prescribed only that "the hat shall not be removed, but shall be tilted on the back of the head, so that as the eater bends over to get his mouth nearer the victuals the hat may still retain an erect position."[16]

Eating house fare likewise reflected this straightforward approach to dining. Proprietors avoided the French-influenced cuisine gaining prominence elsewhere in the city and stuck primarily instead to serving traditional Anglo-American dishes like roasted and boiled meats (most commonly beef, turkey, chicken, and ham), potatoes, baked beans, and sweet pastries. The standard eating house dinner was built on a sturdy foundation of animal protein. Doctors at the time prescribed beef as the most efficient source of energy for working men.[17] Whether it was for health reasons or not, beef was certainly always in high demand at eating houses.

The efficient eating house kitchen precooked as many of the day's offerings as possible in large quantities in order to have any one of them ready the moment a patron ordered it. Slabs of boiled ham and corned beef, big pots of baked beans, piles of biscuits, and trays of pudding stood waiting to be portioned, dished onto a plate, and handed to a hungry customer. Griddles were kept piping hot so that meat sizzled immediately upon touching it. Vegetables like potatoes, peas, cabbage, and turnips were prepared in the morning and kept warm all day in steamer baskets or tepid oil. It is no wonder proprietors complained of having difficulty selling out their day's offering of vegetables; by noontime these vegetables

This *Harper's Weekly* engraving from September 27, 1873, captures a frenzied, chaotic meal in a lower-grade eating house. Charles Stanley Reinhart, "The Lunch Counter."

would have all turned to greasy mush. Patrons ordered their food á la carte (though they certainly would not have used that phrase). Most eating houses could not afford to offer the "all-included" American Plan to hungry working men likely to eat all they could hold, and today's convention of a fixed meal including a meat entrée, vegetable, and starch all listed together on the menu for one price and served on one plate (a "plate dinner") did not exist until the early twentieth century.[18] In the eating house, patrons instead ordered exactly what they wanted and as much or as little as they liked or could pay for.

Though there were undoubtedly eating houses that built a successful reputation based on their fare, overall the quality of food was not what drew men to these venues. Eating house cuisine was routinely derided as some of the worst food in the city, and certainly far inferior to home cooking.[19] Only in jokes about the culinary inaptitude of newly married housewives did it occasionally emerge as superior. And yet men showed up at noontime day after day for their fill of it. For most customers, the convenience and speed of the eating house trumped any complaints they may have had about the taste of the food.

Distinctions among Eating Houses and Eating House Patrons

The male-dominated, no-fuss eating house was thus a distinct genre of nineteenth-century commercial eatery, one that stood in stark contrast to the city's luxury venues. But there was also considerable variation within the genre. Subtle and sometimes not-so-subtle distinctions among eating houses set establishments apart and made some venues more appealing to certain occupation types, socioeconomic groups, races, and ethnicities. *Harper's New Monthly Magazine* in 1866 delineated for its readers the general taxonomy that had developed among eating houses in Boston and other American cities, explaining that prices for "low-class" establishments ranged from six to ten cents per plate, thirty to thirty-five cents for "good class," and twenty-five to sixty-five cents for "best class."[20] Price point, however, was only one of several factors differentiating eating houses in Boston.

Location, surprisingly, did not play as dominant a role in distinguishing among eating houses in Boston as it did in other cities like New York.[21] Boston's docks, where predominately Irish day laborers found intermittent work cutting fish and unloading ships, attracted the lowest-end venues. The particular clientele of these establishments was likewise primarily Irish. Otherwise, downtown Boston was only rather slowly experiencing geographic differentiation among its commercial enterprises.[22] Retail shops, offices, banks, and other businesses generally mixed indiscriminately on Boston's streets throughout most of the 1800s.[23] This meant that different grades of eating houses, appealing to different workers' tastes and pocketbooks, also intermingled throughout the city's commercial hub.[24]

There were wide variations, however, in the kinds of actual space Boston's eating houses occupied, and these differences did help to shape the character of a particular venue's clientele. For example, the lowest, cheapest class of eating house—the kind that attracted the poorest patrons—was often located in a space that was exactly that: low. These venues were frequently little more than a "subterranean," windowless room in the basement of a building or warehouse.[25] Kitchen and dining room were one and the same. These spaces tended to be cramped, as well as poorly lit and ventilated; indeed, their poor ventilation helps to explain the frequency of fires in eating houses, a very common news item in Boston newspapers for most of the century. Poor ventilation also explains one of the most remarked on characteristics of such venues: their smell. Discerning patrons again and again described the pungent aroma of grease and onions, mixed with acrid tobacco smoke and the unpleasant body odors of male patrons who had likely spent all morning performing some kind of manual labor.

As can be imagined, the dining ambience of these basement venues was far from fancy. Instead of sitting at tables, customers typically ate standing up along the counter behind which their food was cooked. This helped to expedite service and eliminated the need for waiters. To accommodate more customers, some establishments also provided one or two communal tables, referred to as "boards," to which patrons could belly up—or at least try to. According to one reluctant patron of a cheap eating house in 1844, "the back-less seats were nailed to the floor so far from [the tables] that the *epicures* who patronized the establishment dined at an angle of forty-five."[26] Silverware was rarely supplied, either because proprietors couldn't afford to purchase it or they worried their patrons would abscond with it. Some customers brought their own utensils, but many preferred to just rely on their hands; pocketknives could also be useful tools for conveying food to mouth. Napkins were unheard of, though toothpicks, by all accounts, were in great demand and available for an extra charge.[27] (In a pinch, the pocketknife could do this job, too.) These venues were often quite dirty, and rarely was much thought given to décor. Mismatched furniture and chipped plates and cups were used without embarrassment, presented to hungry men who were unlikely to notice or care.

The service in these eating houses was equally bare bones. Most proprietors could not afford to hire help with the cooking or waiting and so performed these jobs themselves or with the assistance of family members. Those who did employ additional help paid them very little; by the 1880s, the *Boston Daily Globe* reported that the average pay for male waiters of eating houses was just four to eight dollars a month.[28] At such wages, eating house waiters could not have been expected to be as well trained or to provide as high a level of ceremony and ritual as waiters at luxury hotels.

But while being a waiter in these venues required less polish and training, it still demanded considerable work. Eating houses—even the most wretched ones—could become extremely crowded during the busy noon hour, and most were undoubtedly understaffed as a strategy to keep overhead expenses as low as possible. Besides taking and delivering orders to hungry, hurried men, waiters were tasked with maintaining order among patrons. One Boston newspaper reporter interviewed a waiter who kept a "good-sized" stick of wood, "big enough to make a pretty big bump on a man's cranium," that the waiter referred to as his "persuader" behind the counter for just this purpose.[29] Refusal (or inability) to pay one's bill was one type of trouble waiters frequently confronted. General rowdiness and the occasional alcohol-fueled brawl were others. Sometimes patrons came in already drunk and angry from work; other times the disagreement originated in the eating house itself, as was the case with one "savage fight" the *Boston Herald* reported in April 1857. A group of intoxicated men took to stabbing each other with broken glassware, and, as the newspaper concluded, "considerable bad blood was spilled."[30] Keeping order among such customers was not an easy job, and it was not uncommon for patrons to turn their violence on the waiters, as was the case when John Luckey attacked John Morse, his waiter, on October 13, 1854. Mr. Luckey, the *Boston Atlas* joked, was "lucky enough to get off with $10 and [court] costs."[31] The paper did not report how the waiter fared.

As a result of the low pay and stressful working conditions, waitering in an eating house was a considerably less desirable job than working in a first-class establishment. Remember that 62 percent of Boston's restaurant waiters in 1850 were nonwhite or foreign born.[32] Unfortunately, it is impossible to determine the specific kind of eatery in which a waiter listed in the federal census or city directory worked, and so the precise social makeup of eating house waitstaffs remains elusive. But it is certain that native-born white men would have scorned working in these venues even more than they did establishments like the Tremont. Indeed, even the occupationally limited Irish looked down upon eating house waiters. In 1847, the *National Police Gazette* reported on an uppity, Irish, working-class woman who lorded it over other women in her neighborhood that her husband was a waiter at a nice restaurant downtown while their husbands worked at more plebian establishments.[33] Given the low esteem associated with being an eating house waiter, it is likely they were even more likely to be nonwhite or foreign born.

The significant proportion of Irish working as eating house waiters imparted a distinctive flavor to patrons' dining experiences. According to one bewildered patron, the Irish brogue alerting patrons to the day's menu items sounded something like "Haunchavenision, breastervealand-oysters, very nice; . . . rosegoose, legger-lamb an' sparrowhawks."[34] Further perplexing were the "restaurant calls," a kind of precurser to diner slang, that eating house waiters used. "Boston strawberries" (baked beans), Cincinnati quail (pork), "sleeve balls" (fishcakes, authentically, a piece of fish between two potato slices), and "stars and stripes" (pork and beans) were some of the most commonly used in Boston.[35]

As for the actual fare in these basement eating houses, we cannot know for sure about its quality. It certainly received plenty of criticism, but again eating house fare was generally maligned. One especially infamous specialty was hash, a dish of mixed chopped meat, potatoes, and onions.[36] In the cheapest places, hash was rumored to be composed of all the uneaten bits of food that had been left on patrons' plates and subsequently gathered up, reheated, and served again to someone else. Proprietors of the cheapest venues were also accused of purchasing and serving spoiled meat and rotten eggs because such products could be obtained at a discount, thus padding profit margins. In part, this suspicion of eating house food stemmed from disbelief at these establishments' rock-bottom prices. At Carr's Eating House in the 1850s, a man could feast on roast pork, veal, lamb, or broiled beefsteak for just six cents.[37] When asked, proprietors vigorously denied resorting to any such culinary chicanery to keep their prices this low, insisting instead that they shopped for inexpensive cuts of lean meat that could be cooked carefully to taste good and relied on high volume to turn a profit.[38] They were also careful not to waste parts of animals others may have thrown away—animal organs, flanks, and necks all found their way into eating house fare, if only to help flavor stews and hashes.[39] In a candid interview with the *Boston Daily Globe*, a proprietor of one cheap eating house acknowledged that his patrons were not necessarily concerned about the quality of the food they received: "Our trade is generally hungry. Folks that come in . . . ain't the kind that eats for fun or to kill time. They generally have a good appetite and are mighty glad to get something for it—be it ever so humble."[40] In this venue and in many others like it, food was food.

If a man was willing to spend more on his afternoon dinner—anywhere from just a few cents more to almost a dollar, depending on the venue and what he ordered—he could dine higher up in the hierarchy of eating houses and enjoy certain improvements in style and service. In these more expensive venues, the dining room tended to be larger and aboveground; hence, light and air circulation were better. The kitchen and dining room were distinct spaces, with the kitchen frequently located in the basement below the dining room. For example, when Mr. A. R. Campbell remodeled his eating house on Wilson's Lane in 1850, separating the kitchen from the dining room was one of the primary improvements he made.[41] As a result of this arrangement, the whiffs of cookery were not so intense to patrons as they dined. Separate tables and booths replaced counters and "boards" to provide customers with greater space and privacy.

There were improvements in cleanliness as well, and sometimes there were even pictures hung on the wall or shabby curtains on the windows for decoration.[42] These eating houses further provided such dining accoutrements as silverware and napkins. The "napkin rack" was one innovation that helped proprietors save money on laundry costs by reserving regular patrons' napkins to be reused several times between washes.[43] A customer simply retrieved his designated napkin from the rack each time he visited and returned it after his meal. Finally, waiters were more numerous and thus more attentive. Together, these enhancements served to justify higher menu prices and helped to draw a kind of clientele that could afford to pay them.

But even in these better-appointed and more expensive eating houses, men still ate in a rush, with little regard for decorum or sociability, intent on getting back to work as quickly as possible. In many cases, their patrons were still wage laborers like clerks and other lowly white-collar workers whose dinner breaks were limited in length. Even patrons who were self-employed would have learned by now that time was money. Overall, there was probably not much improvement in the quality of ingredients or cookery in these pricier venues. Instead, there seems to have been a general feeling that they just charged extra for more or less the same poorly prepared, greasy dishes.[44]

So why frequent a higher-priced venue only to receive essentially the same food as that available in cheaper eating houses when the meal was still a rushed, haphazard affair? What was the benefit, particularly if one was a clerk or otherwise still "on the make," with little extra income to spare? By choosing a superior class of eating house and paying more for their dinner, dining amidst clean-swept floors and well-arranged tables,

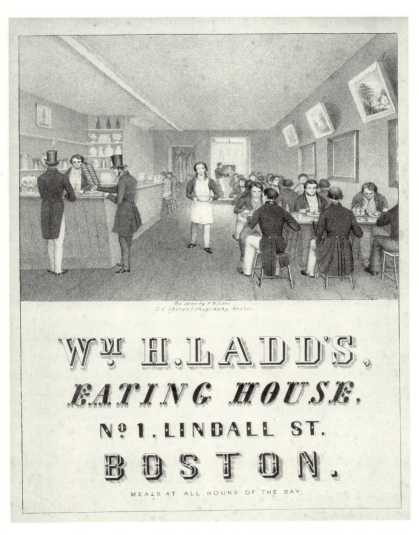

The atmosphere of this eating house is clearly orderly and restrained. *Wm. H. Ladd's Eating House, No. 1, Lindall St., Boston*, Lane lithograph, circa 1840. Courtesy of American Antiquarian Society.

middle-class and aspiring middle-class men asserted their economic superiority over those who ate in the lower sort. But more important, they asserted their cultural superiority. "Loafers" and "rowdies" ate in the lowest venues, kept in line (or not) by the threat of the waiter's "persuader," picking their teeth with their knives and oblivious to the bad odors and filth surrounding them.[45] But in the nicer eateries, middle-class and aspiring middle-class men indicated that they valued virtues like cleanliness, privacy, and the propriety of using a napkin and fork (and not a pocketknife, or worse, their hands) at the table.

Even if their social and economic positions were precarious, as they often were, even if they had yet to secure their economic independence, and even if they barely had time to pay attention to their enhanced surroundings before dashing back to work, dining in these venues instead of the cheaper ones became a kind of cultural capital, a way for a man to demonstrate that he possessed characteristics that prepared him for, and made him worthy of, opportunity, upward mobility, and ultimately success.[46] Though many patrons may have had to choose what they ordered carefully and eat less in order to be able to afford dinners at the nicer eating houses, the fringe benefit of the opportunity to distinguish themselves culturally from those who dined in the lower sort was worth the additional cost. And of course the higher prices these eating houses charged also had the advantage of excluding lower-class, manual workers, the very people with whom many perilously positioned, lower-middle-class customers so desperately did not want to be confused (even though, economically speaking, they may not have been so very different from them).[47]

In this way, the acknowledged hierarchy of eating houses suggested a tacit acceptance among the working and middle classes of the ordering of society and culture promulgated by the wealthy with the opening of the Tremont House dining room. In Boston's growing assortment of restaurants, *what* one ate was important. But even more important was *how* one ate it. Dining out provided a means by which to sort the city's increasingly diverse population and justify that sorting.

The Eating House as Shared Experience

Although highly stratified, Boston's eating houses nevertheless also united Boston men in common experience. Precisely because there was an eating

Bolted Beef and Bolted Pudding

house to accommodate nearly every budget, frequenting an eating house became a daily occurrence for many men, resulting in significant changes in these men's lives. Instead of dining with their families, men in Boston became accustomed to eating among strangers, paying for the convenience with their hard-earned wages. Moreover, eating houses became an integral component of the city's blossoming commercial and market culture. These venues helped make it possible for men to fill their bellies and still submit to their employers' demands on their time.

There were other ways as well in which the city's eating houses helped to collapse and obscure the social divisions among Boston men. There is little doubt that at least some patrons moved back and forth between the different grades of eateries, perhaps dining higher up in the hierarchy of venues on some afternoons and pursuing meals in cheaper establishments on others. Even Benjamin Crowninshield, the wealthy Harvard student we met in the introduction, enjoyed varying the cost and quality of his commercial dining choices.[48] Indeed, the open, competitive nature of the eating house business encouraged men to seek out and try different places for any variety of reasons. Perhaps one afternoon on his way to dinner at his usual spot, a man noticed a particularly enticing daily special scrawled on the door of another venue and decided to step inside. Perhaps clerks favored one eating house when the boss was treating but went to another when dinner was on their own dime. Perhaps some men were willing to spend a bit more on dinner soon after payday but then descended into the basement venues as their pocketbooks gradually emptied. Boston's dining landscape offered male diners the opportunity to make a social ascent or descent as they chose or could afford on any given afternoon.

Even nonwhite Bostonians—a category that included not just blacks but also Irish, Italians, and Jews—found that they were generally welcome in the city's eating houses. For European immigrants, eating houses often provided them their first taste of "American" food. In many cases, this fare, purported (according to one source) to resemble "half-chewed tobacco," was probably not the most ideal introduction.[49] But for men from countries where meat was a luxury, the sight of broiled beefsteak, roast veal chops, and boiled ham all being dished up in plentiful quantities and bolted down by their fellow patrons—and for only a few cents—must have been a wonder.[50] In Boston, even the iconic baked beans were laced with bits of pork.[51] The immigrant patron of the eating house, lined up along a counter with men from various backgrounds, thus began to learn the ways of eating and living in America: abundance was possible, as long as one did not waste too much time on dinner and hurried back to work.

There were some notable exceptions to this policy of inclusivity, however, and they typically involved the city's black residents.[52] Frederick Douglass, for example, reported that he had experienced the early stages of Jim Crow segregation in 1846 when he was told at one eatery, "We don't allow niggers in here."[53] But such strict racial intolerance does not seem to have been the general rule in Boston. As Walt Whitman exclaimed when he visited the city in 1856, "At the eating houses, a black, when he wants his dinner, comes in and takes a vacant seat wherever he finds one—and nobody minds it."[54] His surprise suggests that Boston's eating houses were more welcoming in the antebellum period toward blacks than Whitman's native New York. This observation would be borne out after the Civil War when, in 1865, the Massachusetts' state legislature became the first to prohibit discrimination based on race in public places, including dining venues.[55] Comments Frederick Douglass made as a dinner guest at the Parker House in 1884 indicated that the city of Boston did make real efforts to enforce its postbellum civil rights legislation. According to Elizabeth Hafkin Pleck: "No other northern state passed as many civil rights laws or was as inclusive in its coverage of discriminatory acts as Massachusetts."[56] Nevertheless, there is no doubt that blacks in Boston continued to experience at least some level of discrimination and segregation in public accommodations like restaurants until well into the twentieth century.

Of course, not everyone in Boston experienced eating houses as patrons. For their staffs, eating houses were one of a limited number of racially integrated workplaces in the nineteenth century. As noted, because of the low esteem associated with working in an eating house, their employees tended to come from the polyglot assortment of migrants to the city, especially the African American and Irish populations with few other options.[57] There were instances throughout the 1800s when these inclusive workforces banded together to try to secure goals of shared self-interest. For example, waiters at different venues in Boston repeatedly joined together to strike for higher wages. Late in the century, they also formed the Waiters' Benevolent Association, an interracial mutual aid society. Perhaps even more noteworthy was the network of lookouts that white antebellum Boston restaurant employers and employees developed to warn black waiters—many of whom were fugitive slaves—whenever slave catchers were in the vicinity.[58]

Discrimination was more evident, however, among eating house proprietors. While immigrants from across Europe opened dining venues in Boston (close to 14 percent of Boston's restaurant keepers were foreign born in 1850 and almost 30 percent were born abroad by 1880), black Bostonians were legally prevented from entering this trade until the 1840s.[59] According to British visitor Edward Abdy, "Even a license for keeping a house of refreshment is refused [blacks], under some frivolous or vexatious pretense, though the same can easily be procured by a white man of inferior condition and with less wealth."[60] Later, even once such legal barriers were removed, African American restaurateurs long continued to struggle in Boston. By 1850, the federal census listed just five black restaurant proprietors in the city.[61]

One of them was Joshua Bowen Smith, who operated an establishment at 16 Brattle Street in Cambridge.[62] Smith, known in Boston as the "prince of caterers," was by far the city's most successful black restaurateur. He was also a virulent abolitionist who advocated black pride and self-defense and actively assisted fugitive slaves in Boston. Smith's political activities must have interfered with his professional interests. Most white Bostonians denounced abolitionism and would have expected obsequiousness from black restaurant proprietors. Perhaps this explains why Smith's business by the late 1850s seems to have been limited to catering to abolitionist organizations.[63]

Smith's race eventually hurt his business in other ways as well. In 1861, after feeding the 12th Regiment of Massachusetts Volunteers for a period of ninety days during the Civil War, Smith presented a bill for $40,378 to Governor John Andrew. Andrew, however, refused to compensate Smith, arguing that the state legislature had failed to appropriate the funds with which he could legally make payment. And yet in anticipation of the legislature's later reimbursement the governor had already paid the other proprietors—almost certainly all white men—who had provided similar catering services to soldiers.[64] The state's failure to pay devastated Smith. Though he later recouped a little more than half of the total bill, he was nonetheless forced into bankruptcy. Historian Shane White has recently found that black businessmen like Smith operated with the constant fear that their white customers would refuse to pay them.[65]

Racial discrimination also negatively affected black restaurant proprietors' access to credit. Moreover, in the period before the founding of the national bank system during the Civil War, there was a chronic shortage of specie. Private banks freely printed and put into circulation paper money in an effort to meet this demand. The problem was that counterfeit and "broken" bank notes (notes issued by failed banks) were all too common.[66] As a result, the exchange of money for goods was an extremely fraught process that hinged largely on trust. Once again, black businessmen were at a distinct disadvantage in negotiating this process with white customers.[67]

Racially and ethnically diverse spaces, the heterogeneity of Boston's eating houses could—and did—result in conflict. Racial and ethnic slurs were slung alongside hash. Fights were not uncommon, fueled by a combination of racial and ethnic friction and alcohol. For example, racial tension was evident in an incident reported by the *Boston Daily Globe* involving several Irishmen and an African American man at O'Connell's eating house at 163 Beach Street, a clash that resulted in three broken windows and stitches for one of the men.[68] That time, no one was seriously injured, but these scraps could turn deadly.[69]

Tensions engendered among an interracial eating house staff similarly ended in violence. The surprising frequency of knife and gunfights reported in Boston newspapers between interracial restaurant employees hints at the status anxiety and conflict that often plagued these working relationships. For example, in April 1890, after a long and stressful afternoon of service, a black cook was accused of stabbing a white waiter with a knife, though the cook later insisted to the *Boston Daily Globe* that his weapon had been a broken pie plate and that he had been motivated by self-defense.[70]

Racial and ethnic distinctions never broke down entirely within the walls of the eating house, though they were often transgressed. Thus, eating houses simultaneously—and paradoxically—helped to both define and blur differences among male Bostonians. The range of these venues became a vehicle for signaling and legitimizing difference. But the common experience of bolting an eating house dinner also served to link the separate rhythms of patrons' individual lives to each other and to the city and its economic growth. Above all, eating houses facilitated the demands made by a capitalist economy on traditional patterns of eating. Standing elbow to elbow along the counter, customers of the eating house came to a new understanding of what it meant to be a man living, working, and eating in the city.

The genre of the eating house did eventually meet its demise at the turn of the twentieth century, but not because workers were suddenly given more time in which to seek out and enjoy their midday meal. Instead, throughout the century mealtimes gradually shifted and the main meal of the day was pushed back to later in the evening, after the workday was through, so that families could once again enjoy this meal together. Meanwhile, comparatively lighter afternoon appetites and expectations were increasingly satisfied by a new urban trend: the sandwich shop (and the sandwich cart, its mobile version).[71] And in 1875, after the repeal of a statewide alcohol ban that had stunted (though far from suppressed) the city's liquor trade between 1852 and 1875 (with the exception of brief periods when the ban was temporarily lifted from 1868–1869 and 1871–1873), many Boston saloons began offering a "free lunch" with the purchase of at least one nickel beer.[72] Generally consisting of pickled eggs, crackers, and preserved meats—anything salty to encourage a thirst for more beer—this saloon-marketing technique seriously infringed on the business of cheap eating houses. Finally, as more and more women began to participate in the trend of dining out, men increasingly chose to patronize restaurants where they were more likely to enjoy the company of female diners.[73] Women's growing eagerness to dine out meanwhile invoked other conversations about the meanings and consequences of dining out in Boston.

CHAPTER 3

Charlotte Russe
in the Afternoon

Elite Ladies' Eateries

In *A Tale of Lowell* (1849), the pseudonymous writer Argus tells the story of Julia Church, a millworker who accepts an invitation to go to Boston, "the metropolis of New England," to eat dinner at a restaurant and attend the theater with her handsome young suitor, Caldwell. Julia is dissatisfied with her work in Lowell and dreams of living a life of grandeur in the big city. Caldwell exploits Julia's social ambitions in order to seduce and, ultimately, rape her.[1] Urban consumer pleasures prove central to Julia's ruin, and chief among them is dining out.

In Boston, Caldwell takes Julia on a tour of first-class venues of public consumption. Their first stop is the American House, one of the premiere luxury hotels in the city, where Caldwell buys them dinner. After dinner, the couple attends the theater, and then "Caldwell called with her to Brigham's," another fashionable dining establishment, "and treated her to some oysters." Besides being a beloved New England delicacy, oysters were a long-suspected aphrodisiac. Returning with Julia once again to the American House, he orders them each a mint julep. Julia has enjoyed herself up to this point, delighting in the elite commercial novelties of the city and in being entertained like a lady. But she now learns that Caldwell intends for them to stay in the city overnight and share a hotel room at the American House. According to the novel's narrator, Caldwell "'booked' his name on the register at the office 'Mr. Caldwell and Lady, Lowell.' The clerk, as is ever usual in such cases, casually enquired: 'One, or two rooms, sir?' Caldwell replied, 'One.'" Unable to convince Caldwell to take her home, Julia initially insists he sleep on the sofa while she takes the bed. But the mint julep has weakened her powers to resist his sexual advances. By the end of the chapter, Julia finds herself in bed with Caldwell, "her fate sealed."[2] Left pregnant and deserted, Julia later dies.

A Tale of Lowell, part of a small genre of midcentury novels focused on female millworkers, registered the uncertainty that Americans felt regarding working women's virtue.[3] In this particular story, the moral dilemma posed by Julia's factory work is compounded by her willingness to indulge in commercial amusements like dining in restaurants. For women of any class to eat in a commercial establishment in this period was considered potentially perilous. After all, "true" women were supposed to limit their engagement with the public, commercial sphere. For a woman to dine in the public eye, drawing attention to her body and its various biological processes, was especially risqué. But throughout the nineteenth century, affluent women from well-respected families began to enjoy (within limits) greater autonomy in moving about the city that included dining in a select number of restaurants that were considered appropriate for them to patronize. These women's wealth and family prestige provided them a kind of shield that protected them from the potential dangers of engaging in such activities, at least as long as they pursued them in the proper way.[4] In turn, these ladies' ability to dine outside the home facilitated their further engagement with the public, commercial life of the city. Working women like Julia, however, lacked such defenses. As Julia's story suggests, working women's willingness to participate in commercial pleasures only further undermined their moral virtue. Moreover, because their reputations were not assured, working women's presence in the eateries that so-called true ladies frequented threatened to destroy the precarious propriety of female dining venues altogether.

Elite women's participation in the trend of dining out was made possible partly through the exclusion of lower-class women, at least for much of the century. The dining venues that catered to these well-heeled ladies strove to uphold and reinforce middle- and upper-class gender ideals, including those prescribing women to be sheltered from the male, commercial realm of the city. And yet in responding to women's need for protected public space where they could relax and enjoy a meal, ladies' eateries helped to deepen women's involvement with the public, commercial life of Boston. Along the way, ladies' dining activities became a

Charlotte Russe in the Afternoon 65

vehicle for discussing deeply rooted concerns associated with the experiences of consumer pleasure and conspicuous consumption and gradually helped to legitimize both.

EARLY RESTAURANTS AS PREDOMINATELY MALE SPACES

Since the colonial period, respectable women wishing to patronize a hotel or tavern had to choose their venue carefully. Prostitutes were often present in these spaces, and so women wishing to safeguard their reputations dared not enter. However, a small handful of establishments provided highly regulated spaces to accommodate reputable female travelers and wealthy local women who could attend balls and assemblies there with a male escort.

These circumstances continued among the growing number of Boston restaurants in the early antebellum period. Some, like the main dining room of the Tremont House Hotel, specifically prohibited women patrons in order to prevent any taint of impropriety from their establishment. The vast majority of early Boston restaurants were thus masculine spaces, and they signaled as much through a combination of location, décor, and menu. Nearly all had locations in the downtown commercial district, the political and business heart of the city. Though women were often present downtown—they moved through the area to shop, participated in social and civic organizations, and, with increasing frequency, worked—the area was imagined (at least) as belonging to men.[5] Eating houses occupying dingy basement rooms were further characterized as male spaces because of the association between underground venues and places of ill repute like brothels and gambling dens where respectable women did not go. Dark woods and heavy upholsteries, popular in venues like hotel dining rooms, emphasized the masculinity of these spaces, while the mismatched and shabby décor of many eating houses equally denoted male tastes (or lack thereof). Menus laden with meats like beefsteak and pork were intended to appeal to hearty masculine appetites. And the fact that most establishments served alcohol made them indecent for female patronage since there was a long association between public drinking and commercial sex.[6] Finally, the way many eateries were used to (literally) fuel commercial pursuits or serve as settings for business and political meetings cemented their status as extensions of the male public sphere.

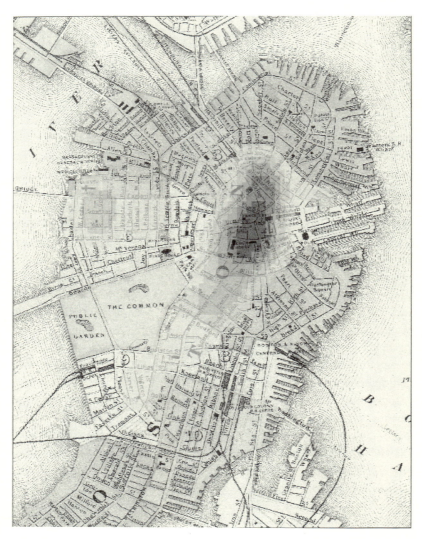

The density of dining venues in Boston in 1850: darker areas indicate a higher concentration of eateries. Image produced with the software ArcGIS; address data for dining venues were gathered from the 1850 Boston city directory.

LADIES' DINING ROOMS AND CONFECTIONERS

Beginning in the 1830s and increasing steadily throughout the century, the growing number of affluent women for whom returning home to eat after a morning spent running errands or attending society meetings was inconvenient or impossible constituted a new potential market of diners. But where could these women dine without compromising their virtue and their reputations? Eateries that catered primarily to ladies, protecting women's reputations and defending their femininity through suitably appointed settings, began to offer viable solutions.

High-end hotels were among the first to meet women's new dining needs. Luxury hotels like the Tremont, Revere, and Parker Houses all contained a "ladies' dining room," separate from the main dining room, where they could eat alone or with friends without undermining their respectability. As with the hotels' main dining rooms, the spaces dedicated to women served both the guests of the hotel and affluent local women of Boston.

As we know, Boston's elite hotels were already polite institutions that filtered out riffraff and drew attention to the respectability and refinement of their patrons. But their ladies' dining rooms took additional precautions to guard the propriety of female diners. These efforts began at the door. The Tremont House, for example, provided a special ladies' entrance at the side of the building for the use of unescorted women.[7] This kept women from having to climb the main steps of the hotel—often occupied by loitering men chatting or smoking—to use the front entry.[8] The ladies' entrance led directly into a specially designated ladies' receiving room, dining room, and parlor.[9] Together, these spaces provided women with their own discrete sphere within the larger world of the hotel, preventing them from having contact with strange men and also shielding them from the hotel's more overtly business and political spaces. Though ladies' dining rooms shared the general downtown location of the hotel, their more specific location within the building was thus securely feminine.[10]

Ladies' hotel dining rooms were carefully designed to be bright and airy spaces, the antithesis of the majority of men's venues. The spacious ladies' dining room at the Tremont House, for example, was outfitted with large plate-glass windows facing Tremont Street that flooded the room with light.[11] Favored window treatments in ladies' eateries like the

Tremont were delicate lace curtains, which allowed dappled sunshine to pass through even when they were drawn. Mirrors and glass chandeliers reflected this light, helping the space appear larger and brighter.[12] All of these design elements conveyed a sense of innocence and transparency, as if nothing untoward could happen here.

Cultural authorities in the nineteenth century believed that women were drawn to environments that reflected their own naturally delicate and beautiful natures. Hotels thus took great care in decorating their ladies' dining rooms and redecorated often in an effort to remain current and fashionable and retain the favor of their female patrons.[13] Plush velvet sofas and chairs and rich carpets created a soft, supple effect, which read as feminine. Floral motifs were common, lending these spaces the feel of a garden. For example, in the ladies' dining room at the Parker House, "a fresco with soft, harmonious tints of yellow, red and blue" adorned the ceiling. According to a newspaper, "the design [of the fresco] is geometrical and rectangular in outline, but the details are filled with conventionalized flowers, leaves, vines and fruits suitable to a room used for such a purpose."[14] Why were flowers considered suitable in a room devoted to feeding women? Women supposedly loved flowers, "an inheritance from Eve."[15] As one authority explained, "Certain it is that her taste for these fair creations has descended to her daughters with very few exceptions."[16] Frescos depicting flowers and fruit thus stood in feminine contrast to the often highly sexualized artwork of nineteenth-century saloons, which might include statues of cavorting satyrs and nymphs or paintings of nude women.

Even the seating arrangements in women's venues were specially designed with female concerns in mind. Ladies' dining rooms contained numerous small tables covered with white tablecloths. These smaller, individual tables were considered more appropriate for women than the large banquet tables found in many male-dominated restaurants (like the main dining room of the Tremont) or the counters in eating houses. Shared eating spaces like banquet tables and counters were seen to risk putting women in compromising social positions since the patrons sitting next to them might be strangers. Counters had the additional drawback of being reminiscent of a public bar.[17] In contrast, separate tables created a gap between those dining at one's own table and strangers at other tables. As historian Jessica Sewell has found, it was perfectly polite in these circumstances to turn one's back on strangers at other tables.[18] Tables thus gave the illusion of privacy even in the public setting of the commercial eatery.

Ladies' dining rooms further demonstrated their suitability for women through their menus. Most important, they prohibited alcohol, thereby unequivocally distinguishing themselves from public drinking places. And compared to men's eateries that emphasized meat, menus at ladies' eateries offered lighter foods, thought to be more suited to women's small and contained—and thereby refined—appetites.[19] As one authority explained, "A woman's appetite is as capricious as coquettes are said to be, and they are fed on as unsubstantial viands as can be picked out of a pastry-cook's shop."[20] Lighter fare like broiled and stewed oysters, sandwiches, poached eggs, boiled ham, omelets, and salads were typical menu items in ladies' dining rooms.[21] There was also an array of sugary items, especially ice creams, chocolates, and fancy French pastries like éclairs, intended to appeal to women's special penchant for sweets, thought to be another feminine trait.[22] Indeed, by the 1880s the *Boston Daily Globe* described the now notoriously sugary cravings of female restaurant-goers with some disdain: "A favorite lunch with the ladies is a plate of soup and ice cream, or pudding, or pie, or charlotte russe. Many women . . . will make a lunch off ice cream and cake, or cake and charlotte russe, a thing a man never thinks of doing."[23] Like the venues that served them, such food choices were considered unmistakably feminine.

These dining establishments were not entirely off-limits to men. To begin with, the waiters were still always male, just as in male-dominated venues. A woman was also welcome to bring a male guest to dine alongside her if she chose, though no such escort was necessary. A man was not, however, permitted in the ladies' dining room unless accompanying a woman. This helped to ensure that all male patrons were respectable acquaintances of female diners and guarded against the presence of strange men in the venue.

Many men found the femininity of ladies' eateries oppressive and considered it a chore to accompany a female friend or relative to one. As the *Boston Daily Globe* explained: "It is rare to see a man in a women's restaurant. When one does come in, no matter under what circumstances, he wishes he had selected some other place."[24] Some men, however, found they missed the pleasant effects and companionship of the ladies' dining room when their party did not include a woman. As English tourist Charles Murray explained in 1857, being turned away from the ladies' dining room meant being "shut out from many privileges, deprived of the most agreeable society, and compelled to mourn your lone estate in company with fellows as wretched as yourself."[25] But it was only through such exclusionary practices that these eateries could strive to guarantee female diners' propriety and comfort.

Over time, the popularity of ladies' eateries led them to proliferate beyond the boundaries of first-class hotels. In the 1860s and 1870s, freestanding establishments catering to women opened throughout Boston's downtown shopping district and later in the elegant Back Bay as well.[26] To underscore their distinction from men's restaurants and suggest their suitability for women (and women's sweet tooths), freestanding establishments often went by the name *confectioner*.[27] Confectioners created a highly feminine environment for their female patrons in much the same way as ladies' dining rooms at hotels.

Confectioners did not, however, have the benefit of a location safely embedded within an already refined hotel. Instead, they relied on being placed on fashionable streets in close proximity to the chic shops women already patronized. The best ones occupied rooms on the street level, since requiring women to go upstairs, lifting skirts above their ankles, was almost as bad as requiring them to descend underground, and "not to be tolerated in good society."[28] Freestanding confectioners were also more likely to take out advertisements in Boston newspapers to alert the public to the suitability of their accommodations for women. For example, Lee's ice cream saloon on Washington Street published sheet music for "The Ice-Cream Quick Step" as a way to advertise.[29] The cover included an elaborate illustration of elegantly dressed men and women enjoying light refreshments and ice creams in a beautifully decorated setting. Mrs. Harrington advertised her ladies' eatery in a city guidebook, as did Marston's.[30] Such marketing efforts suggest that these establishments may not have been considered as obviously reputable as ladies' dining rooms in hotels, though there may have been other reasons—such as cost, convenience, or the quality of their fare—that women chose to patronize confectioners instead.

These strategies for feminizing restaurants continued to serve as the basic model for women's eateries until well into the next century. Indeed,

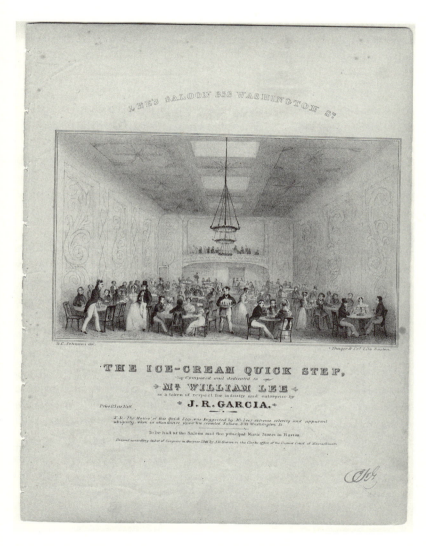

The cover for this piece of sheet music illustrates an elegantly appointed confectioner where women and men dine together. J. R. Garcia, "The Ice-Cream Quick Step" (Boston: J. R. Garcia, 1841), from Library of Congress, Music Copyright Deposits 1820–1860.

72   Charlotte Russe in the Afternoon

with only very minor changes, turn-of-the-century department store lunchrooms, tearooms, and cafeterias—all of which similarly courted a mostly female patronage—adopted the same basic approach to providing safe and feminine dining space pioneered by hotels and confectioners in the antebellum period.[31]

THE PLEASURABLE GREGARIOUSNESS OF LADIES' EATERIES

For well-heeled ladies on the go, restaurants promised the same convenience of providing a place to dine away from home as they did for working men. For such affluent women, many of whom lived on the suburban outskirts of Boston, dining out was usually part of a full day spent shopping, attending lectures, or going to organization meetings in the city. For example, before becoming a restaurateur and owner of the esteemed Parker House Hotel, Harvey Parker worked as a coachman for a wealthy Watertown woman. He recalled that his employer's frequent shopping trips into Boston always included a stop at a favorite eatery where she would refresh herself before completing the day's errands.[32] Antislavery and women's suffrage activist Caroline Healey Dall recorded in her diary how dining out became integrated into her reform activities in Boston. One afternoon, she wrote that she "took a light dinner at Parker's" after hearing a variety of speakers at a meeting of the Massachusetts Anti-Slavery Society.[33] Another day she stopped at the Tremont House for dinner before "attending [Swiss zoologist Louis] Agassiz' first lecture on the Plan of Creation."[34] Some female political and social associations even began using women's eateries as spaces in which to hold their meetings.[35]

But in contrast to most men, affluent women also had the expendable time and resources to make dining out in the middle of the day a truly enjoyable, leisurely activity. Indeed, unlike in eating houses, where men ate in a rush to get back to work and made little to no time for sociability or pleasure, contemporaries often remarked on the great gregariousness of female dining venues. "What an array of moving jaws engaged in either conversation or mastication!" exclaimed an observer.[36] A proprietor of one venue explained that his typical customer "spends an hour or more at the table chatting with her friends about the weather, the fashions, the opera, her servants, children, dentist, dressmaker, poodle and sometimes even her husband."[37] Another stated, "Women really take more satisfaction out of their meals than men, spending more time over them and rarely eating alone."[38] Clearly, the affluent women who patronized ladies' dining venues found them pleasantly convivial in addition to merely convenient.

And why not? These women's membership in a privileged class afforded them both the income and leisure time necessary to enjoy an unhurried meal while men worked and lower-class women either worked or took care of children. (Children rarely seem to have accompanied women to ladies' eateries, suggesting that the women who were most likely to dine out at midday also had access to child care.) Indeed, the relaxed, chatty atmosphere of female dining venues further helped to distinguish them from men's restaurants and associated these venues even more firmly with the refined and the feminine.

Few women, however, patronized ladies' dining establishments for the evening meal. In fact, freestanding ladies' eateries did not even remain open after dark, as no respectable woman would have ventured out past this time unescorted.[39] Ladies' dining rooms at hotels did continue to provide evening meals, but these extended hours were primarily intended to accommodate the female lodgers of the hotel. Even they were encouraged to take their meals in their rooms after a certain hour. As late as 1904, at least one etiquette guide admonished women: "A lady should never go alone to the supper table after ten o'clock. If she returns from an entertainment at a late hour, and has no escort to supper, she should have that meal sent to her room."[40] Dining out in the daylight was acceptable, but dining out after nightfall—because of lingering associations with prostitution—was not.

ANXIETIES ASSOCIATED WITH FEMALE DINING VENUES

Women's eateries were thus designed to be bubbles of feminine space in the midst of the otherwise masculine and potentially dangerous world of the city. Here, women could dine alone or with friends in comfort and style without fear of impropriety. Even etiquette manuals—typically rather conservative when it came to gender norms—assured women that such eateries were perfectly acceptable for them to patronize. As one author advised, women should feel free to take refreshment in "respectable public restaurants" during the day without male escort, although it went on to suggest that "two ladies should if possible be together rather than one."[41] And yet despite their rather conventional intention to shield

74 Charlotte Russe in the Afternoon

women from the potential hazards of the public, ladies' eateries nonetheless posed some surprisingly powerful challenges to nineteenth-century gender ideals and values.

For example, ladies' dining space was not always used in the gender-specific way for which it was designed. When Englishwoman Marianne Finch attended a dinner at the Revere House in 1853, she ate in the protected space of the ladies' dining room. But separated from the men's dining room by only a Venetian screen, Finch reported that she and her fellow female diners quickly "became cognizant of all that was passing on the other side of the screen."[42] Finch's anecdote is illustrative of the way in which ladies' eateries—intended to shore up gender boundaries—could nonetheless assist women in transgressing them.

Indeed, by providing public havens, semisegregated though they may have been, where women could refuel themselves, ladies' eateries allowed women to extend the time they spent away from their prescribed sphere, the home. By giving women space where they could publicly indulge their appetites to consume, ladies' dining activities also undermined practices of consumption, existing since the revolutionary period, that sought to curb women's economic and social power by calling for them to avoid commercial activities and shun display.[43] Thus, although ladies' eateries professed to protect women from the dangers of the city and the market, they actually deepened their participation in both.

As a result, women's dining venues threatened to empower women and overturn traditional gender roles that subordinated them to men. In order to reverse these dangerous trends, midcentury women were instructed to avoid the restaurant and return instead to their own kitchens to prepare wholesome meals for their husbands and families (or at the very least oversee their servants' preparation of these meals, since the women who were most likely to dine out at midday were also likely to have domestic help). Indeed, in prescriptive literature like women's magazines and household guides, the home-cooked meals women prepared and served took on sacred qualities; they became symbolic of feminine virtue and a salve to the ills of modern, commercial society. According to one authority:

> The gathering together of the members of the family, after the morning's separation . . . re-awakens the domestic sentiment and inclines to social pleasure. The worry of business and the anxieties of personal responsibility

yield to the delights of companionship and the soothing effects of mutual sympathy.[44]

Writers implied that if women shirked their duty to cook and dined in restaurants instead, their own dissipation and the dissipation of their families would surely be the result.[45]

As if this were not enough, critics of women's commercial dining activities also chided and mocked female diners for the poor decisions they made in restaurants as consumers. Indeed, women were accused of everything from utter incompetence in making up their minds about what to order at restaurants, to ordering too little (thanks to their peckish appetites) and wasting the time of their (male) waiter, to an inability to control their outrageous sweet tooths.[46] A shared assumption behind all these critiques was the idea that commercial activities like ordering at a restaurant were better left to men. "It's such a bother to order," the *Boston Daily Globe* quoted a woman customer saying to her friend in a ladies' eatery. "I wish Papa was here. He doesn't have any trouble."[47] These appraisals of female diners belittled and denigrated the potential power the role of consumer gave them.

Women who dined in restaurants were further accused of licentiousness. At its most paranoid, the critique of women's commercial dining activities in popular culture ignored the special precautions that ladies' eateries took to guard the virtue and guarantee the respectability of their female patrons and assumed instead that these venues were really dens of vice and iniquity. Moralists and reformers, for example, suggested that the special appeal for women of dining unescorted was the freedom it gave them to drink and cavort away from the presence of their husbands and families. Never mind that women's eateries intentionally prohibited the sale of alcohol in an effort to create an appropriately feminine and chaste atmosphere. These venues were nevertheless accused of disguising liquor in supposedly nonalcoholic drinks and creating an environment in which women could get drunk where their families would not find out.[48] Even more troubling was the allegation that women used eateries for illicit encounters with men. According to one observer, "Yonder are a middle-aged man and woman in deep and earnest conversation. They are evidently man and wife—though *not each other's!*"[49] Admonitory literature explained that it was easy to assume that the male guests women brought with them to ladies' dining rooms and confectioners were their relatives—most likely a husband, a brother, or a father—but in the "anonymous hall" of the public restaurant, how could anyone be certain these relationships were genuinely virtuous?[50] This, of course, is precisely the situation in *A Tale of Lowell* when Julia enters the American House on the arm of the philanderer Caldwell.

Accusations such as these threatened to undo the careful ways in which ladies' eateries had established themselves as public venues that were nonetheless safe for respectable women to patronize. The severity of the indictments against female diners and female eateries suggests just how radical it was for women to dine in these spaces. It is likely that the public moralists who condemned women dining in public were not so much describing peoples' true beliefs about what regularly went on in women's eateries as they were lending a voice to Americans' worst fears about the effects of urban anonymity and commercialization on the country's morality. After all, at the heart of the nation's moral center was its placement of women, which made their abandonment of the domestic sphere a fundamental challenge. These critics lashed out against an increasingly popular practice that they disapproved of but were unable to stop.

ELITE WOMEN DINERS HELP LEGITIMIZE CONSPICUOUS CONSUMPTION

Even as Bostonians and other Americans voiced anxiety over the consequences of women's growing participation in dining out, women's patronage of dining venues was paradoxically also something restaurateurs were eager to draw attention to. A proprietor hoped that if the word got out that his restaurant was respectable enough to win the patronage of the elite women of Boston, even more Boston women would visit without fear of compromising their reputations or virtue and with the hope of partaking in these women's fashionableness.

Indeed, leveraging an existing female clientele to encourage additional female patronage made good business sense. Restaurateurs thus strove to showcase their female patronage, advertising their venue's suitability for and popularity among well-heeled women in the city's society press.[51] Conveniently, the large windows with which many ladies' dining venues were fitted not only helped to create a light and airy atmosphere but also allowed passersby to see the stylish women enjoying themselves inside. Here again we see ladies' eateries straddling a thin line between claiming to shield women from the public sphere and facilitating—even drawing attention to—women's involvement and delight in it.

Female patrons must have felt the various tensions that characterized their dining activities. In some ways, it is surprising that so many of them still proved willing to navigate the potential hazards eating out posed. Evidently, the pleasure and freedom dining in a restaurant gave them proved worth the complications and complexities. It is also true that the elevated class and status of female diners continued to provide a kind of armor against these dangers. Throughout the nineteenth century, elite women were the absolute arbiters of virtue and taste.[52] They could thus challenge the rules of polite society (within certain limits) without serious risk to their reputations. In fact, their actions and decisions could even help to modify these rules.

This is precisely what happened within the realm of dining out. Though anxieties about female diners lingered, an eatery that attracted a refined female clientele signaled that it had achieved the highest level of propriety. Over time, this logic helped Bostonians become more comfortable with the pursuit of consumer pleasure and luxury, not only for women but also over protestations that conspicuous consumption would lead to a dissolute and idle republic.

Indeed, by the 1860s and 1870s, proprietors and managers of luxury hotels even began welcoming women to dine in their main dining rooms so long as they were properly escorted.[53] Women's introduction to these spaces undermined the carefully constructed masculinity of these venues that had been originally intended to reconcile anxiety over the potentially feminizing levels of opulence they provided. But by this time Americans had grown more comfortable with conspicuous consumption, in no small part because women had joined in. What was more important now, especially considering the heightened competition among the proliferating number of refined restaurants, was for a venue to establish itself as the *most* fashionable. Well-heeled women's patronage was central to this endeavor.

Of course, this change in policy meant that hotels had to make some significant alterations to their main dining rooms. Banquet tables gave way to individual tables at which separate parties could dine in semi-privacy. (This adjustment was also facilitated by the growing popularity

This image shows men and women dining together in the main dining room of the elegant Crawford House, another Boston luxury hotel. *Boston Daily Globe,* June 17, 1875.

among dining venues of serving meals at all times as opposed to regular, set times.) Décor was refreshed and lightened. Male patrons were reminded to abstain from smoking and drinking (beyond wine) with ladies in the room; consumption of harder beverages moved to the hotel bar. Men were also encouraged to devote more of their meal to making pleasant conversation with their female companions and to limit talk of business and politics.[54]

Not all male patrons were happy about these transformations. According to one gentleman: "Ladies come late and dishes are spoiled by the delay. They take up no end of place and get their skirts under your chair. They don't eat, and men are ashamed to devour beside them . . . then also ladies are apt to sit too long at dessert, encouraging its senseless profusion, and they frown upon the cigar."[55] Nevertheless, women's presence at the public table—and in the public more generally—was here to stay.

NONELITE WOMEN AND COMMERCIAL DINING

The conveniences, pleasures, and potential transgressions of ladies' dining venues were not equally available to all women. To the contrary, these venues had to be carefully policed at all times in order to make sure that women whose reputations were at all suspect (for example, working-class women like Julia Church) were not present. Restaurant proprietors thus routinely inspected women who wished to dine in their establishments to make sure they were "respectable" enough to join their other refined patrons.[56] Tunis Campbell advised hotel managers to perform such inspections in 1848: "Ladies who may be traveling alone should not be left to come to the table without being seen by the proprietor and brought in and seated."[57] Women who somehow did not measure up were turned away; otherwise their presence risked besmirching the character of the truly virtuous female diners in addition to the venue itself. High prices and the expectation that diners perform complex dining rituals further served to exclude working-class women. Finally, since these venues do not seem to have welcomed children, potential patrons also required access to child care, another expense.[58]

Middle-class women probably had the resources and could command the respectability to be able to indulge themselves with visits to a confectioner or hotel dining room at least occasionally. To pinch pennies, they may have chosen a slightly less fashionable venue where the menu prices were lower or preferred to order just a dish of ice cream or cup of tea as a special treat and not a full meal. Newspaper interviews with waiters confirm that groups of female diners often tended to be very cost conscious. One waiter explained that his female patrons

> always ask for the bill of fare and read the figures first. Men, you know, say, "Do they cook oysters decent?" but she always says, "What do they cost?" . . . When I give the check they count up everything by itself, and say, "Oh, mercy did the cake cost all that?"[59]

As annoying as this behavior may have been to their waiters, middle-class women had to order carefully to ensure they stayed within their budgets (especially because they rarely controlled these budgets).

Another, very different way that a smaller number of middle-class women became involved in the business of dining out was to become restaurateurs. Just as it was now proper for them to frequent a ladies' eatery, it was also reputable for a woman to operate one, as long as it catered to other respectable women. Newspapers and periodicals even recommended proprietorship of a ladies' eatery as a way for women— especially widows—to "earn pin-money" without "losing social caste."[60]

Antebellum female restaurant owners are elusive for historians to identify because census takers did not record occupational information for women before 1870. City directory canvassers rarely recorded occupational information for women either, and the business section typically listed proprietors only by their initials instead of their full names, sometimes adding an honorific "Mrs." or "Miss" but not consistently. Nevertheless, a careful examination of the Boston city directories, census records, and Certificates of Married Women Doing Business reveals the names of numerous female dining venue proprietors throughout the 1800s.[61] In 1870, the first year the federal census recorded women's occupations, 21.1 percent of the restaurant proprietors it listed were female.[62]

It was extremely difficult, however, for these female restaurateurs to stay in business. The high rate of failure among female proprietors partly reflected the difficulty of the restaurant business itself and the high competition between eateries.[63] But as the credit evaluations of R. G. Dun make clear, for a woman to succeed as a restaurant owner required overcoming even greater odds stemming from special prejudices regarding the capabilities of her gender. For example, Dun evaluators frequently noted in their reports the hard work and creativity of Boston's female business owners. And yet because of their gender, these evaluators were generally willing to extend to these women—at most—only "a very modest credit."[64] As a result, female proprietors faced a higher rate of failure than their male contemporaries.

For working-class women, excluded by a combination of price and custom from venues that catered to elite women and men's eating houses, dining out was extremely rare for most of the century. Working-class women's prohibition from the city's dining venues was not especially problematic in the antebellum period. Compared to elite and middle-class women, women from the working class were less likely to require midday commercial dining options. Instead of shopping or going to the meetings of reform societies during the day, these women worked or took care of children at home. The majority of those who worked labored in domestic environments performing sewing or millinery outwork or acting as house servants. There was rarely a reason women so employed could not also eat in these domestic work settings. In fact, meals were often included as part of a house servant's wages.[65]

This situation began to change in the last decades of the 1800s, as women's employment opportunities expanded and women workers found themselves in downtown factory and office environments similar to men. Still, working women were more likely to carry food with them to work or when out for other reasons due to their exceptionally low pay.[66] These female workers occasionally supplemented their meals from home with cheap, ready-made items purchased from pushcarts, groceries, bakeries, and delicatessens.[67] There were also some eating houses that began to reverse their policies of banning women. Some put up signs indicating that they now welcomed female patrons.[68] But it seems few women chose to patronize these establishments given their still typically rude environments and clienteles and the fact that most of them continued to serve alcohol.[69]

Besides, by the end of the century, mealtimes and diets were changing. The demands of an industrial economy had by this time pushed the main meal of the day back into the evening, after the workday was through. Gender norms were changing, too. Working-class men and women now began to embrace a new kind of restaurant venue where they could dine together as part of their evening's commercial leisure activities. This genre was known as the café.

CHAPTER 4

Roast, Chop Suey, and Beer

Cafés

By the second half of the nineteenth century, dining in restaurants had become a way of life in Boston, not merely for convenience or even necessity—not just for novelty or entertainment—but for all of these reasons. So many new restaurants! The biggest increase late in the century was in the number of cafés. Cafés were venues that stayed open late into the evening to serve a mixed-gender crowd after the workday was through. With the growth of new immigrant communities after 1870, the diversity of cuisines available in Boston's cafés expanded considerably. By 1894, an article in the *Boston Daily Globe* richly described the cafés in Boston that now served up ethnic fare, including German, Italian, and even Chinese.[1] The article made clear it was not only immigrants who ate in these venues; the city as a whole had begun to at least tentatively embrace ethnic food and ethnic cafés as part of an urban food culture increasingly defined by its commercialism and variety.

CAFÉS MEET NEW DINING DEMANDS

In the second half of the nineteenth century, there was even greater demand for commercial dining options in Boston than in the first. New dining needs stemmed from a combination of interrelated factors. Among the working and lower-middle classes, the most important contributor was the large increase in the number of young men and women residing in lodging houses, particularly by the 1870s and 1880s.[2] According to economist Albert Benedict Wolfe, who later published a study of Boston's lodging houses, Boston had more such housing than any other city with the exception of San Francisco.[3]

Lodging houses rented out kitchenless rooms and, in contrast to boarding houses, did not provide meals, leaving their residents largely dependent on restaurants.[4] Lodging proved popular late in the century because lodgers felt they could live more frugally by seeking meals in the city's cheap restaurants and paying only for what they actually ate rather than having to pay for board up front, as in a traditional boarding house.[5] Dining in restaurants also afforded lodgers greater flexibility to dine when and where they chose, and with whom they chose. Thus the spread of lodging houses was made possible by the expansion in restaurants earlier in the century. In turn, lodging stimulated additional restaurant growth since lodgers continued to need affordable places to eat. Between 1861 and 1890, there was a 200 percent growth in the number of restaurants listed in the *Boston Business Directory*.

Boston's lodging houses were most densely clustered in the once-genteel South End, the heart of which was the intersection of Dover and Harrison Avenues. This was a lively, crowded area of Boston and, by this period, one of the city's most diverse.[6] According to a resident, here the South End's "multifarious business bursts through the narrow shop doors, and overruns the basements, the sidewalk, the street itself. . . . Its multitudinous population bursts through the doorsteps, the gutters, the side streets, pushing in and out . . . all day long and half the night besides."[7] The South End was where Boston's Chinese population settled; it also gradually replaced the West End as the city's largest black enclave.[8] To house this "multitudinous population," landlords carved up the interiors of the South End's swell-front brick houses—former single-family residences—into rooms, which they rented out for a few dollars a week to factory and dockworkers, shop girls, clerks, and other working and lower-middle-class people.[9] Though the South End itself was diverse, lodging houses were less likely to mix races and, as historian Sarah Deutsch notes, some also discriminated based on other qualifications like religion. Lodging houses did, however, contribute to a developing, heterosocial youth culture in the South End, since single men and women rented rooms in the same building. Married couples also resided in lodging houses, though families with children were rare.[10]

A shift in mealtimes that recast dining as a leisure activity among the working and middle classes, as it had long been for the elite, was another factor that helped to fuel greater restaurant demand. Throughout the

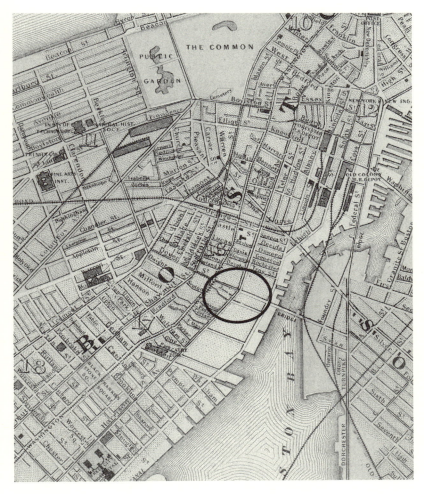

Plan of South Boston, 1880, showing the intersection of Dover and Harrison Avenue, the heart of South Boston. Norman B. Leventhal Map Center, Boston Public Library.

century, the requirements of a regulated industrial work schedule steadily pushed the main meal of the day back until later in the evening, after the workday was finished.[11] Now during the part of the day classified as "leisure," working- and middle-class Bostonians began to look for ways to combine the necessity of eating with commercial entertainment and sociability.[12] Restaurants provided this opportunity. At the same time, dining in restaurants became coupled with the enjoyment of other commercial amusements like theater and, by the early twentieth century, dance halls.[13]

In addition to generating greater demand for restaurants among the working and middle classes, these changes also raised these populations' expectations of their restaurant dining experiences. Men continued to patronize eating houses and the free lunch counters of saloons for quick afternoon "lunches." Delicatessens and a growing trade in pushcart delicacies like oysters, watermelon, and ice cream provided even quicker, less inexpensive options.[14] But for leisurely evening dinners, Bostonians sought out dining venues that stayed open late and provided a more relaxed and sociable dining environment in addition to good, moderately priced food. Above all, there was a new expectation that restaurants accommodate women as well as men, as the separate-sphere ideology of the nineteenth century began to give way to the mixed-sex social interactions of the twentieth.[15] Young, single working women, likely to pinch pennies when it came to lunch by carrying food with them to work or by skipping the meal entirely, were eager for male companions to "treat" them to dinner.[16] Married middle-class women frowned on these unchaperoned activities among their lower-class sisters.[17] But they too wanted mixed-gender restaurants now that the later dinner hour meant that middle-class couples and families could dine out together after husbands returned home.

BOSTON'S DIVERSE CAFÉS

Cafés became popular because they fulfilled the new dining expectations of the working and middle classes. Located along major thoroughfares in the downtown residential districts, cafés were usually cleaner than most eating houses and provided better service and more elaborate settings in which men and women could enjoy their meals. To guarantee their respectability for female patronage, many took the precaution of prohibiting alcohol from their menus, as elite ladies' eateries did.

Café prices were inexpensive; a complete meal generally cost between just fifteen and fifty cents.[18] The cheapest venues were located below ground, many in the basements of lodging houses.[19] According to the records of R. G. Dun & Company, a nineteenth-century credit-rating service, maintaining such low prices meant that many cafés operated on razor-thin profit margins. Indeed, Dun investigators regularly evaluated café proprietors as "risky" for credit, describing them as "probably not making much over a living," or "not supposed to be making much money," or—at best—"slowly making a living." But the Dun records also indicate how important patron loyalty was to the success of a restaurant, and to cultivate that loyalty proprietors had to set prices low.[20]

One strategy that proprietors used to keep their overhead costs down was to hire female "waiter girls"—also known as "table girls" (*waitress* seems to be a term coined in the twentieth century)—to serve guests instead of male waiters because they could pay women less than men. The *Boston Daily Globe* reported in 1883 that women waiters made between two and four dollars per day, which was two to four dollars less than what male waiters working in comparable venues earned.[21] The same article also reported that roughly half of the city's restaurant waiters were now women. Elite venues and male-dominated eating houses still refused to employ women as waiters, so the majority of the city's waiter girls worked in cafés.

Female waiters promised additional benefits to café proprietors besides their willingness to work for low wages. Some restaurateurs hired women because they believed women would be less sexually threatening to their female and family patrons than male waiters. Other proprietors, however, actually hoped that waiter girls would contribute to an exciting, sexually charged dining atmosphere; these proprietors sought to hire especially attractive women and encouraged them to flirt with male customers.[22] Rarely did proprietors hire both men and women for their waitstaff; coed staffs were frowned on.

Native-born whites and Irish immigrants were preferred as waiter girls. A newspaper article in January 1883 profiling the city's female restaurant waiters claimed: "Almost half [of the city's female waiters] are natives of the United States or of Ireland, perhaps a sixth of the whole member being . . . among other nationalities. Of these two there is a slight preponderance in favor of the Irish, and of those who are natives of this country a large majority are Irish-Americans."[23] The article did not mention a single instance of a black female waiter. Indeed, it was very rare for black women to labor in this kind of work, though they found similar jobs in private homes as domestic servants.[24] The exact reasons for black women's lack of participation as waitstaff in restaurants are not clear but likely included discrimination against them by proprietors and patrons and, perhaps, hesitation on the part of black women themselves to work as restaurant waiters since waitering remained one of the best-paying, menial occupations available to black men.[25] Within the black community, black women's entry into the occupation would have risked undermining the elevated status of waitering for men.

In his 1881 novel *A Modern Instance,* William Dean Howells described the straightforward service and setting of a typical café in his adopted hometown:

> The plates were laid with a coarse red doily in a cocked hat on each, and a thinly plated knife and fork crossed beneath it; the plates were thick and heavy; the handle as well as the blade of the knife was metal, and silvered. Besides the castor, there was a bottle of Leicestershire sauce on the table, and salt . . . the marble was of an unctuous translucence in places, and showed the course of the cleansing napkin on its smeared surface. The place was hot, and full of confused smells of cooking; all the tables were crowded, so that they found places with difficulty, and pale, plain girls, of the Provincial and Irish-American type, in fashionable bangs and pull-backs, went about taking the orders.[26]

Clearly, the venue Howells described was not fancy, but the red doilies suggest an effort at least to create a homey atmosphere. Individual tables provided patrons a feeling of privacy as they ate. Some cafés also offered counter service, which single men were still more likely to take advantage of than women, couples, or families.

Cafés sold meals following two different models: at some establishments, individual dishes were sold à la carte. Others provided table d'hôte meals. The café's table d'hôte meal was more modern than a traditional tavern's. Café proprietors did not heap food upon a table and expect guests to help themselves to whatever they wanted. Instead, for one set price, café patrons received a multicourse meal, with the courses served one at a time. (Some cafés did maintain, however, a center table where rolls, biscuits, lettuce, butter, vinegar, salt, and pepper were piled for patrons to take all they wanted to supplement whatever they ordered.) The courses usually consisted of soup or salad, a meat or fish dish, and dessert. Guests chose what they wanted for each course from a bill of fare. One popular business strategy among cafés in Boston was to sell tickets that entitled the purchaser to multiple table d'hôte meals at a particular venue, usually for a slightly discounted price.[27] This ensured the patron's loyalty to the venue, for at least as long as the meal ticket lasted.

The most ubiquitous type of fare served in late-nineteenth-century cafés was traditional, stick-to-the-ribs New England cuisine. For example, in the venue Howells described, a "great show of roast, and steak, and fish, and game, and squash and cranberry-pie" sits in the café window, enticing customers in from the street. Inside, patrons dine on "hulled corn and milk" or baked beans, a particular Boston favorite.[28] Typical dishes at similar venues also included chicken salad, rump steak, oysters, fried fish, and roast beef.[29]

After 1870, as Boston's immigrant population became more diverse, Boston's selection of cafés expanded to include those that offered German, Italian, and Chinese foods.[30] Boston's immigrants clustered in ethnic enclaves throughout the South and North Ends.[31] Owned by immigrants themselves, the "ethnic cafés" in these neighborhoods catered primarily to fellow immigrants by providing a familiar taste of home and a sense of community with which to dine. Staples of ethnic cuisines often included cheap cuts of meat that took considerable cooking time to make palatable. Ethnic cafés provided this effort so that busy working immigrants with inadequate cooking facilities did not have to do so. Restaurants also sourced foreign ingredients that individuals may have had difficulty accessing.[32]

The cuisine available in a particular kind of ethnic café was often more complicated and varied than native-born Americans realized. In Boston as in other U.S. cities, immigrants from different regions of their home countries blended together to form an "ethnic" group. Regional identities, customs, and cuisines typically became less distinct in America, but they did not disappear entirely. For example, most Italian immigrants to Boston came from the southern regions of Campania and Sicily. In the so-called "Italian" North End, there were sections where immigrants from specific regions clustered: the Sicilian section, for example, or the Avellinese section.[33] The cafés in these areas specialized in providing the kind of cuisine that would most satisfy the palettes of the patrons in their specific neighborhood. The same was true of German cafés, with some venues specializing in Bavarian fare, others in the comparatively lighter seafood dishes of northern Germany.[34]

German immigrants had been settling in Boston since the colonial period, and German cafés were among the first ethnic restaurants in the city. By the final third of the century, these venues were concentrated in the South End. German cafés were notoriously plain in décor but otherwise clean and pleasant. Their proprietors sprinkled sand or sawdust on the floor to facilitate easy cleanup of the restaurant once it had closed for the day. Dishes like rinderbraten (roast beef), herring salad, and rye bread were basic to their menus. In German table d'hôte cafés, the price of a meal typically included soup, a choice of meat, bread, and a glass of beer. As in other ethnic cafés, the codes governing women and alcohol were less severe; in fact, German families felt no compunction about bringing their children to these cafés, or, according to some sources, even in giving them beer to drink.[35] Live music was often part of the fun at German cafés as well.[36]

Italian cafés became prevalent in the 1880s and 1890s with the growth of Boston's Italian population. They were scattered throughout the South End but clustered most densely in the North End, an Italian enclave after 1870.[37] These venues catered especially to bachelors; Italian families were more likely to dine at home for both cultural and economic reasons.[38]

The interior of a German café, as depicted in William Dean Howells, *Their Wedding Journey.* Note the woman drinking beer.

Italian cafés tended to be even plainer and cheaper than German cafés, a reflection of Italians' inferior economic position in Boston in this period. They were often hidden inside Italian grocery stores, where the "shelves are filled with bottles of olive oil and packages of dressing for fish and game. Oddly shaped cheeses are strung along the shelves and hang suspended from the ceiling." Just past the "barrels and boxes of rice, macaroni, and spaghetti" was the restaurant proper. Italian cafés promoted a communal dining atmosphere by installing "long and narrow" eating tables "roughly made of wood and covered with cheap oilcloth." Lace curtains and exotic displays of fruits and vegetables decorated the windows. In one venue, "immense bowls filled with spaghetti" cost just ten cents. A glass of wine was ten cents more.[39]

Boston was also home to several Chinese cafés. The city's Chinese community was founded around 1870 in the South End along the northern end of Harrison Avenue between Essex and Beach. It began with several laundries and grocery stores. A handful of restaurants quickly

IN AN ITALIAN RESTAURANT.

This illustration depicts Italian immigrants eating spaghetti in an Italian café. "Boston's Foreign Restaurants," *Boston Daily Globe,* January 7, 1894, 24.

followed.⁴⁰ As in other ethnic cafés, the atmosphere of these establishments was generally simple but clean. "A plain wood floor, swept and scrubbed hourly till it fairly shines; simple pine or walnut tables, [surrounded by] small stools" was the description a Boston newspaper gave of one Chinese eatery in 1885, challenging American stereotypes of the Chinese as inherently dirty.⁴¹ One corner of the restaurant might hold a pile of pillows, inviting customers to lounge and smoke.⁴² The prices in Chinese cafés were the cheapest of all. The fare generally consisted of Chinese vegetables like kohlrabi and eggplant, preserved fruits, pickles,

The interior of a Chinese restaurant, as depicted by the *Boston Daily Globe* in 1889. Note the cat, dog, and mice hanging in the window. Frank Carpenter, "Cooking in Asia, How the Chinese Prepare Their Dishes," *Boston Daily Globe*, November 17, 1889, 18.

seafood, and fried minced meat, all served with noodles or rice and washed down with tea or rice wine. More special Chinese delicacies like bird's nest soup were also available for those who could afford such treats.[43]

Less common but still present in late-nineteenth-century Boston's dining landscape were cafés specializing in Polish, Hungarian, and kosher foods.[44] There were also venues that combined American fare with a particular ethnic specialty. For example, a restaurant at 431–2 Congress Street served "real India Curry" every Tuesday and Thursday in 1872, but otherwise dished up a traditional New England menu.[45]

Despite the number of Irish immigrants in the city, cafés specializing in traditional Irish foods were hard to find. This was not because of lack of Irish participation in the restaurant business.[46] According to historian Hasia Diner, the dearth of Irish cuisine in this period probably had more to do with the starvation so many of the Irish experienced prior

Illustration of Chinese immigrants eating with chopsticks. "Chinese Cooking," *Boston Daily Globe,* July 19, 1885, 9.

to immigrating to America, which had obliterated positive associations with the foods of their homeland. As a result, food was not a marker of ethnic identity for the Irish as it was for other immigrant groups. Most Irish-owned restaurants consequently served up conventional Anglo-American fare.[47]

Boston's small number of black-owned restaurants left few records behind, and it is thus difficult to reconstruct the experience of dining in one of these venues.[48] Did any of them feature the distinctive cuisine that would later be identified as "soul food"? Given the city's significant population of ex-slaves late in the century and this population's concentration in the South End, it is quite possible that at least one or two cafés specialized in the foods with which ex-slaves would have been most familiar.[49] Such foods are, of course, part of the foundation of soul food.[50] But regardless of the particular dishes they offered, Boston's black-owned restaurants continued to experience a high rate of failure, which is one reason, no doubt, that evidence of their existence is fugitive. Historian Elizabeth Hafkin Pleck estimates the chances of success for black-owned service industry businesses in Boston during the last three decades of the century as "at best two in three and at worst, one in three."[51] Whereas Stephan Thernstrom has attributed that failure to cultural deficiencies within the black community, Pleck suggests that blacks' insufficient capital investment and access to credit were the real culprits.[52] In addition, the intense economic discrimination that African Americans continued to face meant that black Bostonians were less likely to be able to afford dining out than other groups and therefore unable to give patronage to the businesses owned by their fellow people of color.

NATIVE-BORN BOSTONIANS' NEW INTEREST IN ETHNIC CAFÉS

Though originally intended to appeal to discrete tastes of newcomers, the growing variety of cafés in Boston soon provoked the curiosity of American-born Bostonians, who became interested in the novel foods and customs on display in ethnic venues. After all, nowhere else was such intimate access to immigrant life available. What did the foreign arrivals to their city eat? How did they eat it? Native-born Americans were eager to use ethnic cafés as windows into immigrants' cultures. According to one newspaper, restaurants provided "an excellent opportunity . . . for the study of human nature."[53] Boston's newspapers capitalized on readers' growing interest in foreign cafés and sent their reporters into these establishments to offer richly descriptive reports. As Bostonians read about these restaurants from the comfort of their own homes, they may have begun to feel more confident about visiting for themselves. Moreover, they began to realize that the city's cafés provided filling, tasty food for an especially low price.

Given the considerable levels of xenophobia in America in this period—xenophobia that culminated in the passage of America's first laws restricting immigration including the 1882 Chinese Exclusion Act—the sudden interest in ethnic foods among white, native-born Bostonians might seem surprising. Indeed, Americans had long disparaged the foods that immigrants ate. In 1866, for example, *Harper's New Monthly Magazine* described German food as "greasy and dirty."[54] Meanwhile, Americans derided Italian fare for its heavy-handed use of garlic and spice and reliance on cheap cuts of tough and stringy meat.[55] Chinese food was even more abhorred as consisting primarily of vermin and domesticated animals like dogs and cats that Americans considered more appropriate as pets than food. The *Boston Investigator* traded in such unflattering assumptions about Chinese cuisine in 1854 when it published a bill of fare from a fictional Chinese restaurant that included "cat cutlet, griddled rats, dog soup, roast dog, and dog pie."[56] Such negative stereotyping of ethnic fare was a common way that native-born Americans registered their discomfort with the influx of immigrants into their country.

In other respects, though, Bostonians' increasing willingness to broaden their appetites late in the century was not so surprising. After all, America had an extensive history of cross-culinary contact and influence reaching back to the earliest days of colonial settlement.[57] Moreover, foreignness had come to carry a certain level of cachet when it came to matters of the table. Of course, French cuisine and culture remained de rigueur. But historian Kristin Hoganson has found that after the Civil War Americans increasingly embraced a growing "cosmopolitanism" in many aspects of their culture, including what they ate. This new sense of cosmopolitanism valued culinary interactions with the wider world, and most of all, Bostonians took pride in the growing culinary diversity of the city.[58]

Thus, while the primary clientele of ethnic cafés in this period remained immigrants, native-born Americans gradually became more adventurous in trying them, too. Working-class men, first lured to immigrant neighborhoods for their gambling, prostitution, and, in the case of China-town, opium dens, began to stay for the cheap and hearty food.[59] (Men with any railroad experience out West may have already been at least somewhat familiar with Chinese fare and dining habits.)[60] Epicures and upper-class adventure seekers meanwhile sought out ethnic restaurants because they promised a taste of the rare and the exotic. A writer for the *Boston Daily Globe,* for example, reported on an elaborate dinner party he happened to stumble upon involving "the cream of society eating Chinese viands in a Chinese restaurant, served by Chinese waiters and breathing in soulful Chinese music." The guests included prominent Bostonian writers, academics, and artists. They dined on bird's nest soup, boned duck, and dozens of other Chinese delicacies. The reporter re-counted his great surprise at seeing such an affluent crowd at a Chinese café, suggesting that they were not the regular patrons of such a venue.[61] A Chinese dinner may have been good for a lark, but Boston's elite still preferred the more refined "ethnic" French cuisine of the city's first-class establishments.

Instead it was middle-class Bostonians—often discontented with their existing dining options—who had the greatest incentive to experiment with ethnic cafés. In theory, the clean, moderately priced American venues should have satisfied middle-class dining needs. After all, these cafés were respectable enough even for women to patronize, affordable, and served the kind of traditional New England foods Bostonians knew and loved. But many middle-class dining patrons nonetheless found themselves disappointed with these options.

William Dean Howells captured this feeling of disappointment in his novel *A Modern Instance.* Bartley and Marcia have recently eloped and moved to the city from the Maine countryside. The couple is lower-middle class at best, but they have come to Boston to "seek their fortune." Marcia is excited to dine at a restaurant for the first time. At the same café with the red doilies described earlier, she orders stewed chicken, and Bartley requests roast turkey. They end their meal with thick slices of cranberry pie. To Marcia, the meal is "very good and sufficient."[62] But to Bartley the entire experience is embarrassingly provincial. He longs to take his wife to dine at the urbane and worldly Parker House instead, vowing to do so as soon as he can financially manage it.

Unfortunately, for aspiring men like Bartley, venues like Parker's were just too expensive and exclusive. As we have seen, the attainment of refinement and luxury in venues like Parker's, as well as in a new elite favorite in Boston, Ober's Restaurant Parisian, was a shifting goal. Dining rituals—and menu prices—became especially ostentatious late in the century. As historian Andrew Haley has convincingly demonstrated, even when middle-class patrons had saved enough money to be able to afford a special dinner at an elite restaurant, they typically felt unwelcome and uncomfortable eating there due to their lack of familiarity with its French menu, inexperience in refined dining practices, and, above all, their limited pocketbooks.[63] Nevertheless, middle-class diners like Bartley sought the experience of feeling culturally savvy and sophisticated, an experience the typical American-style café did not provide. Thus middle-class Bostonians found themselves in search of new dining options, and they increasingly turned to the city's growing range of ethnic cafés.[64]

ETHNIC CAFÉS AND CULINARY ADVENTURE

In ethnic cafés, native-born, middle-class Bostonians discovered new tastes and experiences. They learned the gustatory pleasures of everything from herring salad and rye bread to spaghetti and minestrone, to rice and oolong tea. Newspapers that had previously condemned these foods now began assuring readers that they were actually quite delicious. Reporters even allayed concerns about the "strange smells" known to waft from foreigners' kitchens, arguing that once readers had tasted the food from these kitchens, they would no longer mind the smells.[65]

Perhaps most surprising was Bostonians' willingness to cautiously embrace Chinese food. Once again, newspapers both facilitated this process and chronicled it. Reporters assured potential white patrons of Chinese restaurants that, all existing stereotypes of Chinese food to the contrary, they would find many of Boston's Chinese eateries clean, the service polite and attentive, and the cuisine tasty. Moreover, they would find other people like themselves—white, native-born Americans in search of a good, filling meal for a moderate price—already inside enjoying themselves. As the *Boston Daily Globe* explained in 1885:

> The average American when he first approaches the Chinese table does so in fear and trembling. Vague presentiments of ragouts and rats, mayonnaise of mice and similar luxuries float through his mind. Nine times out of ten he leaves the table with the conviction that he has learned

something, and that the almond-eyed sons of the queue are the best cooks in the world.[66]

After this enthusiastic introduction, the reporter went on to demystify the curious table settings that diners would find in the typical Chinese restaurant: "Two ebony chop-sticks, a porcelain spoon, a tiny liqueur bowl, and a saucer filled with a chocolate fluid called se-yu [soy]." The writer helpfully explained that this last item—known to us as soy sauce—was "a hybrid between salt and dilute Worcestershire sauce." Next, the reporter praised the fare, which was served as a succession of courses. It included cold roast chicken; fresh fish and rice; chicken soup; roast duck; dried fish; steamed chopped pork; macaroni and chicken; "dainty dumplings filled with spiced hashed meats"; and, finally, what quickly became Americans' favorite Chinese dish, "chow-chop-sue," better known as chop suey. The reporter enthused, "All the dishes are well cooked and served." He also marveled to his readers that such a large and delicious meal—which included wine or ale—was incredibly cheap.[67]

Here was a meal that was satisfying and affordable. It was also interesting and unusual. Best of all, it incorporated specialized knowledge of both cuisine and custom, particularly regarding the use of Chinese chopsticks, which Bostonians found fascinating.[68] Not every American-born patron was willing—or able—to trade their conventional knives and forks for chopsticks. But many were eager at least to give chopsticks a try. As one diner reported, the first time he ventured to a Chinese café he was "resolved" to eat with chopsticks or "spend the day in learning how."[69] Bostonians expressed similar fascination at the peculiarly Italian "art" of twirling spaghetti around the fork rather than cutting it.[70] As one American diner in an Italian eatery explained: "It was a delight to watch these [Italian] men eat spaghetti. They lifted the slippery, writhing strands of it to their lips with a carelessness and ease that to the Americans looking on seemed simply marvelous."[71] These foreign modes of eating were strange but captivating to Americans. By mastering them, native-born diners demonstrated their own adaptability and experienced the small thrill of learning a new skill.

For those less willing to embrace chopsticks (or fork twirling, for that matter), proprietors of ethnic cafés were more than willing to provide special accommodations—including forks and knives—in an effort to make their American-born customers feel more comfortable in their restaurant and to secure their lucrative patronage.[72] Proprietors also tweaked their menus, toning down the amount of spice and garlic they incorporated into their dishes, in an effort to please American expectations and palettes.[73] Such willingness to accommodate and please their patrons helps explain why ethnic venues became especially popular among a middle class unaccustomed to commanding such service at more elite venues. As they Americanized their restaurants to appeal to American tastes, immigrant proprietors themselves hoped to experience upward mobility into the middle class.

This desire to cater to American diners is evident in the reporter's account of the Chinese café. The prodigious size of the meal the reporter described was not at all representative of the typical way the Chinese actually ate. Indeed, later in the article, the reporter acknowledged that the Chinese patrons of the restaurant did not partake of the same foods as the "whites" but, rather, limited themselves to simpler and more conventional dishes like rice, a small piece of fish or chicken, and tea.[74]

Moreover, Americans' favorite Chinese dish, chop suey, was not authentically Chinese. Invented in America, chop suey, as described by one Boston reporter, was "a ragout of chicken liver, lean pork, bamboo tip, celery bean-shoots and onion," held together by a translucent "gravy" and served over white rice.[75] As a historian of Chinese cuisine has surmised, "You could call it a fried Chinese hash."[76] American diners were crazy for it in the late nineteenth and early twentieth centuries, and generally unaware that it was native to America rather than China.[77]

While business-savvy ethnic proprietors endeavored to cater to American palettes, they redecorated their often plain interiors with more "artistic productions" imported from their home countries in an effort to play up the restaurant's exotic, foreign ambience. For example, a café in Chinatown replaced its simple light fixtures with "iron-mounted lanterns, octagon in form, with cut-glass eyes and distorted metal dragons about their edges" to give the dining space a more "oriental" flair. Another venue boasted tables "imported direct from Canton." In this same venue, "banners of oriental subject make gay the walls."[78] As a final touch, some proprietors hired musicians to play "soulful" foreign melodies for their guests to enjoy as they dined.[79] This attention to décor and atmosphere combined to make American patrons of ethnic cafés feel like they had visited a foreign country. According to the *Boston Daily Globe*, "in these restaurants, glimpses of the life and customs of countries far across the sea could be caught."[80] This was an especially attractive illusion for the middle class in a period when foreign travel was generally reserved for the wealthy.[81]

Ethnic restaurants provided opportunities for the affluent to travel between social worlds as well, and to observe and even engage in risqué behavior among the poorer and less orderly members of society. For these reasons, middle-class and wealthy women only went to such venues properly escorted. But once inside, the illusion of being in another country tended to loosen codes of behavior, even among women. For example, respectable women had long refrained from drinking alcohol in public. But in the ethnic café, they felt free to temporarily abandon these restrictions and perhaps even order a glass of beer or wine.[82]

The opium trade associated with Chinese subcultures in urban America provided an even more exotic diversion. Well-heeled Bostonians trekked to cafés in Chinatown—infamously home to opium dens in addition to restaurants—partly in the hope of catching sight of opium addicts.[83] Others wanted to try out the drug for themselves. Indeed, Chinatown quickly garnered a reputation as a rowdy part of Boston and a center of "demoralizing" activity. According to the Boston police commissioner, the restaurants in this part of town were "as active at 1 or 2 a.m. as at midday. Sometimes there was a perfect babel about 3 a.m." Interestingly, he blamed all this activity on white "slummers" "out on a racket," arguing that "the Chinamen themselves are very quiet and orderly and seldom give us any trouble." The police commissioner added that he was especially concerned about the effects such "rackets" had on the young, tastefully dressed females he saw go into Chinese restaurants on the arms of young men. He worried that they came to Chinatown out of mere curiosity but ended up indulging "beyond eating of chop sooy."[84]

Boston's ethnic cafés gave their American-born diners opportunities to interact with foreigners in a more innocent and constructive capacity as well. The reports that emerged from these interactions were often quite favorable toward immigrants. For example, the *Boston Daily Globe* explained that thanks to the outgoing nature of their German-born employees and patrons German eateries generally had a feeling of *"gemutholichkeit,"* [sic] or "utter friendliness." The same article referred to the

Chinese individuals one was likely to encounter in a Chinese eatery as "welcoming" and "hospitable," while patrons of Italian venues "have always a charm."[85] Overall, ethnic cafés helped to make cultural differences seem enjoyable and thrilling, which elsewhere may have been threatening. In contrast to the period's calls for immigrants' exclusion or assimilation, patrons of ethnic cafés relished (literally) the existence and maintenance of cultural differences within the dining venue. It was precisely these differences that contributed to the cosmopolitanism the middle class and others were seeking to establish by daring to dine in these establishments in the first place.

THE ETHNIC CAFÉ: CULTURAL BRIDGE OR CULINARY IMPERIALISM?

By the 1890s, Boston's number and range of ethnic cafés had become points of civic and national pride. For example, an 1894 headline in the *Boston Daily Globe* proudly declared that in Boston there was "No Need to Go around the Globe to Learn What Others Eat." The newspaper joined a growing chorus of voices in Boston and other major cities with increasingly diverse dining landscapes in suggesting that the complexity of America's culinary offerings was a distinctively American characteristic that should be touted and celebrated.[86]

Bostonians' willingness to embrace ethnic cafés and cuisines suggests that a restaurant could act as a bridge, bringing cultures together.[87] And yet the period was still one of intense hostility to foreigners themselves, especially those of Asian descent. Indeed, the same newspapers that praised Boston's Chinese restaurants also offered plenty of evidence of hostility toward Chinese people in Boston.[88] It is difficult to know which part of this paradox to highlight: that in a time of ethnic tension, at least some Bostonians were willing to set aside their prejudices and try foreign foods; or, that embracing this food and—at least in some instances—the people who served it did so little to ease American xenophobia. In thinking about this question, anthropologist Lisa Heldke has argued that eating foreign food has long been a form of "cultural imperialism." Diners— colonizers—"set out in search of ever more 'remote' cultures" to "co-opt, borrow from freely and out of context, and use as the raw materials for their own efforts of creation and discovery."[89] In other words, eating at a foreign restaurant primarily buttressed the cultural and political power of white American diners, not of immigrants.

In further support of this position, historian Samantha Barbas has pointed out that interacting with immigrants in the subservient roles of cook or server within the clearly bounded space of the ethnic café posed little threat to turn-of-the-century white Americans, while interacting with these foreigners in mainstream economic and social settings often did.[90] Barbas argues that this realization helps to explain why dining in foreign restaurants had such a small effect on lessening American prejudices beyond the arena of the café. She also notes that Chinese food only began to be popular in America after the passage of the Chinese Exclusion Act in 1882, which by strictly limiting the number of Chinese into the country went a long way toward containing the Chinese "threat," perhaps making Chinese food "safe" for native-born Americans to eat.[91] Thus while Bostonians' growing enthusiasm for foreign food was to some extent progressive, ultimately the political consequences of culinary adventurism were limited.

FOOD REFORMERS VERSUS CULINARY ADVENTURERS

Ethnic food did not find universal favor in Boston. On the contrary, the same period that witnessed the growing popularity of ethnic cuisine also experienced the revival of a specifically New England regional culinary identity that lashed out at the infringements ethnic foods and consumerism had made on the American diet. The Colonial Revival Movement expressed nostalgia for a simpler past when the national menu was more homogeneous and prepared and eaten at home. Followers trumpeted the tasty wholesomeness of traditional New England dishes like baked beans and pork, creamed codfish, Indian pudding, Boston brown bread, and clam chowder, all cooked over the domestic hearth.[92]

The home economics movement of the late nineteenth century, which used the guise of science to try and bend immigrant and working-class diets to its own ethnocentric tastes, represented another rejection of ethnic and commercial foods.[93] The city of Boston played a key role in this movement when, in 1879, the Women's Education Association formed the Boston Cooking School.[94] From its suite of rooms at 158 Tremont Street, this organization endeavored to teach working-class and immigrant women how to apply the Yankee tradition of plain, frugal living to their cooking, advocating boiled potatoes over saurkraut, and baked beans over spaghetti. The next year, the school opened a second branch in the North End to be closer to the immigrant populations they hoped to serve. Similar goals resulted in 1890 in the establishment of a "public kitchen" in Boston known as the New England Kitchen. This organization sold takeaway portions of basic New England staples like boiled haddock and "Health Bread" to working-class Bostonians for their private home consumption.[95]

A central premise behind both the Boston Cooking School and the New England Kitchen was that immigrants and other impoverished Bostonians could become better assimilated into American culture and have a better chance of social mobility if they learned to eat traditional American foods. According to home economists and other food reformers, there was a correct and an incorrect way to eat, and immigrants tended to err. Indeed, home economists dismissed ethnic fare as unclean, lacking in nutrition, and generally unfit as part of an American diet. They endeavored to provide immigrants with a better model of how to eat.[96]

Home economists were also very critical of the consumer society America had become by the turn of the century. To these reformers, home cooking continued to symbolize the love of a wife and mother. Home-cooked meals indicated that a woman was doing her prescribed duty to keep the domestic sphere untainted from the public, commercial one. Home economists worried that the restaurants proliferating in Boston signaled the demise of home cooking. Even worse, they feared that the city's restaurants threatened the institution of family itself.[97] The Boston Cooking School thus endeavored to help poor and immigrant women improve their cooking skills in an effort to convince Bostonians to go back to dining at home. Even the New England Kitchen intended the precooked portions of food it sold to the public only as a temporary solution, a template of how the women who purchased them should themselves begin to cook.[98] Moreover, the developers of the New England Kitchen rejected the idea of a dine-in restaurant because they believed that restaurants disrupted home and family life. Their food, they concluded, should go to families and not the other way around.[99]

Both food reformers and the "culinary adventurers" who curiously ventured into ethnic cafés came primarily from Boston's white, native-born middle class. And yet their respective approaches to dining and consumerism stood in stark contrast to one another. The men and women involved in these food reform movements longed to minimize cultural differences in their city and curb consumerism.[100] Culinary adventurers, on the other hand, were eager to experiment with the diversity of cuisines available in Boston's restaurants. Furthermore, they embraced the possibilities of defining themselves by what they purchased, using the exotic meals they bought at restaurants to signal their worldliness and sophistication. They believed that their willingness to enter exotic ethnic cafés and test out the strange foods for sale indicated their special savvy in navigating the urban consumer world in which they now lived.

In other ways, though, Boston's middle-class culinary reformers and adventurers were not so far apart in their ideology. After all, both groups desired to enhance their own power through eating: reformers by telling foreign "others" that their own way of eating was best; adventurers by seeking out ethnic food and venues in order to feel more urbane, influential, and wealthy. Both reformers and adventurers used food as a vehicle through which they could experience a heightened sense of their own Americanness. Reformers accomplished this by proclaiming their class-based approach to cookery as the wellspring of American values and a jumping-off point for assimilation into American society. For adventurers, as the historian Kristin Hoganson has observed, publicly consuming ethnic food and participating in ethnic culture was not unlike "playing Indian" or putting on blackface. Enjoying chop suey or twirling spaghetti in an ethnic café "enabled [diners] to show that they were so fully American they did not have to prove it."[101] In addition, reformers and adventurers alike longed to transform others: reformers by remaking working-class and immigrant diets according to their own ethnocentric and class-based preferences; adventurers by using their greater purchasing power to bend certain aspects of ethnic cafés more to their liking or expectations.

Above all, food reformers and adventurers shared an understanding of the United States as representing modernity and progress. But whereas reformers' vision of progress hinged on a melting pot approach to Americanization (with "traditional" white Anglo-American culture imagined as a redemptive force), culinary adventurers came to believe that what was truly distinctive and definitive about American cuisine and culture was the (relative) accessibility and astounding variety its consumer society engendered. What better evidence of this was there than the astounding diversity of restaurants in cities like Boston?

With the groundwork thus firmly laid in the final third of the nineteenth century, Americans' willingness to eat ethnic cuisine, and even to define America's culinary heritage by the tremendous array of foods its peoples ate, came to full fruition in the twentieth century.[102] In time, the popularity of ethnic fare would even crack the hegemonic hold that French cuisine had long held on American appetites.[103] Today, how many fine-dining restaurants are Italian, Japanese, or Indian? The building blocks of America's culinary DNA now include all of these cuisines and cultures, and many more besides.

By the end of the nineteenth century the growth and popularity of Boston's restaurants signaled the deep changes the city's residents had experienced in their everyday lives as Boston transitioned from a port town to a hub of the nation's powerful market-capitalist economy. Just a generation before, Bostonians had eaten nearly every meal at home with their families. Now nearly all residents dined out at least occasionally, purchasing food and eating it among strangers. Besides meals, Boston's restaurants provided space where Bostonians could test out new social relationships and explore new kinds of public, consumer behaviors. In so doing, Bostonians and the restaurants they patronized had helped to create a new urban American culture.

EPILOGUE

Ice Cream at
Howard Johnson's

In 1929, Boston's mayor Malcolm Nichols and the conservative New England Watch & Ward Society banned Eugene O'Neill's Pulitzer Prize–winning but controversial play *Strange Interlude* from being performed in the city. Boston's Theater Guild thus moved the production to the Quincy Theater in Quincy, Massachusetts, a suburb immediately south of Boston. Thousands of curious Bostonians made the trek to Quincy to see the play that season. Since it was an extremely long show, averaging more than five hours, there was a scheduled dinner break about halfway through. During this intermission, theatergoers flocked to a newly opened restaurant just across the street from the theater in Quincy Square that offered daily dinner specials and delicious ice cream. That restaurant was the first Howard Johnson's.[1]

Howard Deering Johnson (1897–1972) was born in Boston. In 1925, he bought a small pharmacy in the Wollaston neighborhood of Quincy. He quickly found that the most profitable part of his business was the soda fountain, from which he served ice cream prepared from a special recipe that contained double the butterfat of typical ice cream. To capitalize on the steady stream of customers this treat enticed into his store, Johnson added fried clams and grilled hot dogs to his menu. In 1929, he opened the full-service restaurant in Quincy Square, strategically located at a busy intersection facing both the theater and city hall and surrounded by a thriving shopping and business district. From here, he continued to dish up his famous ice cream, along with traditional New England fare like oven-braised short ribs and chicken salad. Johnson soon won the patronage of Quincy's businessmen during the day and families in the evening.[2]

In 1935, Johnson came up with a novel business idea to take his restaurant's success to a new level: the franchise. In exchange for a fee, Johnson allowed other restaurant proprietors to use the name, design, logo, menu, recipes, and supplies of his successful Howard Johnson's. By the end of 1936, there were thirty-nine franchised Howard Johnson's dining venues. Three years later, in 1939, a total of 107 Howard Johnson's existed, most of them poised to take advantage of expanding motor traffic thanks to their locations along America's developing East Coast highways. Patrons learned to spot a Howard Johnson's, or "HoJo's," from the highway by the restaurants' iconic orange roofs, cupolas, and weather vanes. Together, these HoJo franchises generated a yearly revenue of more than $10.5 million.[3]

The appeal of the restaurant franchise concept that Johnson helped to pioneer was that no matter which venue they patronized, customers knew they would find familiar foods, clean environments, and good service at an affordable cost. They knew that they could bring their children without fear of exposing them to impropriety. This kind of reliability and brand recognition, untethered from a specific location, marked a significant change in consumer culture as the socially fragmented world of nineteenth-century consumption gave way to a more homogeneous, twentieth-century mass culture dominated by national corporations like Howard Johnson's.[4] Restaurants were influential in the emergence of a public consumer culture in the 1800s; they now played a critical role in this culture's transformation.

In this book we have examined the rise of restaurant dining in nineteenth-century Boston in an attempt to better understand the tremendous economic, social, and cultural upheavals in urban America in this period. The cultural experience of dining out both reflected and shaped the social relationships and power dynamics of one urban population experiencing the vicissitudes of an increasingly market-driven economy. As Bostonians sought new venues in which to fete important visitors and showcase their refined table manners, as they bolted down a plate of hash or broiled beefsteak at an eating house or ordered ice cream from a confectioner, as they experimented with chopsticks at a Chinese café, they also tested new social mores, consumer behaviors, and gender

This advertisement from *Life* magazine in 1951 extols the virtues of Howard Johnson's famed twenty-eight flavors of ice cream, in addition to its other affordably priced menu items. The advertisement includes the iconic orange-roofed architecture of the Howard Johnson's chain of restaurants.

conventions. Restaurants, clearly segmented along class, gender, racial, ethnic, and other lines, helped Bostonians become more comfortable with deepening social stratification in their city and young republic, even as the experience of dining in a restaurant, an experience that urbanites from across the socioeconomic scale shared, contributed to an emerging public consumer culture that would dominate a century later, as evident in the national popularity of HoJo's and other chains.

Boston has the honor of being home to many firsts in the history of restaurant dining. After all, it was in Boston where the first restaurant in America, Julien's, was established in 1793. The Tremont House Hotel, America's first luxury hotel, was also founded in Boston, as was the Parker House, a trailblazer in replacing the old American style of serving meals only at prearranged times with the more flexible and modern European mode of allowing customers to order food at any time of day. The Boston Cooking School and New England Kitchen, leading food-reform movements of the postbellum period and each highly critical of the trend of commercial dining, were both born in Boston. Finally, in the twentieth century, there was HoJo's, and with it the concept of the restaurant franchise and the incorporation of American appetites.

Firsts are often just that: firsts. They carry little or no historical significance, except perhaps to the antiquarian. It is certainly true that Boston's nineteenth-century restaurant culture, as impressive as it was, was quickly outstripped by New York's. But these particular firsts, Boston's firsts, helped to launch a revolution in dining and critically shaped how it played out. As Boston's appetites changed, so changed the appetites of the nation.

Acknowledgments

I have often imagined taking everyone who has helped in some way with the completion of this book out to a celebratory dinner. It would be given banquet style, like dinners at the Tremont House were, and I would raise my glass many, many times in gratitude to the people who made this book possible.

I must first thank Jonathan Prude, who has long modeled for me how to be a scholar, teacher, mentor, and writer. From him I learned to ask the interesting questions and to answer them with an eye to detail and complexity, in addition to good storytelling. His unwavering support during the hardest parts of researching and writing—not to mention job hunting—kept me going.

Additional intellectual debts are owed to my undergraduate advisor, K. Austin Kerr, at The Ohio State University. Dr. Kerr helped make the big world of Ohio State a tight-knit community, but he also made sure I took advantage of every academic opportunity a school that size offers. At Emory University, the comments of my dissertation committee members Leslie Harris and James Roark undoubtedly made this a better book. I owe thanks to many others at Emory, particularly folks from Woodruff Library. Thank you, Jana Lonberger, Erin Mooney, Robert O'Reilly, Marie Hanson, and Michael Page for your advice, assistance, and technical know-how at many critical junctures along the way. My fellow Prude-advisee Marni Davis was my history guru at Emory from day one, helping me navigate many challenges. I am further grateful to Mary Cain at Agnes Scott College and Larry Youngs at Georgia State, both of whom took me under their respective wings and gave me courage and confidence as a teacher and scholar. Marta Crilly at the Boston City Archives went above and beyond in providing research assistance. And while she may not remember it, historian Cindy Lobel was awfully nice to me one summer when we briefly met at the American Antiquarian Society. It was my first research trip, and she helpfully shared her bibliography from her own research on American foodways.

The Massachusetts Historical Society and Clements Library at the University of Michigan supported my research financially and gave me the opportunity to explore their rich collections. The Laney Graduate School at Emory University provided summer research support. A Mellon Graduate Teaching Fellowship extended my time in graduate school to finish researching and writing my dissertation while I figured out how to transform my academic interests into teaching ability.

I am extremely proud that the University of Minnesota Press published this project. The Press took an early and critical interest in my work beginning in 2011, when I was invited to the Minnesota campus as part of the Thursdays at Four lecture series at the Institute for Advanced Study. Since then, Pieter Martin has been wonderfully supportive and patient and has offered a wealth of sage advice. I am indebted to my peer reviewers Jessica Ellen Sewell and Andrew Haley, two historians whose work I admire very much. Haley's thoughtful and provocative comments and criticism enabled me to turn this into the book I hoped it could be.

At Washburn University, my extraordinary colleagues in the department of history have helped me realize the delights of an academic career. Tom Prasch read every single word of the manuscript and gave thoughtful criticism of its ideas and prose. Kerry Wynn has been incredibly charitable with sharing her ideas and passion for teaching as well as motherhood, while Rachel Goossen has provided much-needed professional development expertise. She has also been a good friend. Robin Shrimplin, Kim Morse, Bruce MacTavish, and Tony Silvestri make coming to the office a pleasure. Outside the history department, Vanessa Steinroetter and Courtney Sullivan pushed my analysis in its final stages. Tom Averill cotaught a class on food and dining that was a whole lot of fun. I also thank my students at Washburn, who everyday help me make new insights regarding this nation's history.

Jackie Gold Hritz requires a special shout out for her friendship. I knew from early on that whatever came of my graduate degree, graduate school would have been worth it for introducing me to her. I was right. And as far as damn good friends go, Brent Uhrig certainly is one.

Finally, deepest gratitude goes to my family. To my parents, Mark and Kathy Erby, thank you for always championing me in my endeavors and making sure I know how proud you are of me. I dedicate this book to you. To my mother-in-law, Lin Schad, I am thankful to have you in my life. To my husband, David Dumbauld, thank you for being my partner and for supporting me in my passions—history and teaching. I love you and count myself very lucky to be your wife. And to my son, Litton Dumbauld, I am so happy you are here! I adore being your mother and I cannot wait to see what comes next.

Cheers!

Notes

INTRODUCTION

1. Benjamin W. Crowninshield, *A Private Journal* (Cambridge, Mass.: Riverside Press, 1941), 52–58. Crowninshield's diary is full of entries noting his commercial dining experiences throughout the three years he kept it.

2. Alice Morse Earle, *Stage Coach and Tavern Days* (New York: Haskell House Publishers, 1968). Snacks (often free ones) were provided by some taverns.

3. Even by the 1840s, 92 percent of the population lived within the 1,100 acres that constituted Boston proper. Richard A. Meckel, "Immigration, Mortality, and Population Growth in Boston, 1840–1880," *Journal of Interdisciplinary History* 15, no. 3 (Winter 1985): 406; Oscar Handlin, *Boston's Immigrants, 1790–1880* (Cambridge, Mass.: Harvard University Press, 1991), 15.

4. David S. Heidler and Jeanne T. Heidler, *Daily Life in the Early American Republic, 1790–1820: Creating a New Nation* (Westport, Conn,: Greenwood Press, 2004), chapter 4.

5. Stephen Mennell, *All Manners of Food: Eating and Taste in England and France from the Middle Ages to the Present* (Oxford: Basil Blackwell, 1985).

6. For general overviews of the market revolution and the social changes it caused, see Charles Sellers, *The Market Revolution: Jacksonian America, 1815–1846* (New York: Oxford University Press, 1994); Sean Wilentz, "Society, Politics, and the Market Revolution, 1815–1848," in *The New American History,* ed. Eric Foner (Philadelphia: Temple University Press, 1997), 61–84; and Jack Larkin, *The Reshaping of Everyday Life, 1790–1840* (New York: Harper & Row, 1991).

7. Handlin, *Boston's Immigrants,* 1–24.

8. Ibid., 72–87.

9. Ibid., 74.

10. Foreign immigrants came in several waves to Boston during 1840–1880. These waves crested in 1849 and again 1854, before subsiding with the approaching

116 Notes to Introduction

Civil War. Once the war was nearly over, immigration picked up again. Steady rates of growth peaked in 1870 and 1873 before falling off abruptly with the coming of an economic downturn the next year. In 1845, foreign-born Bostonians and their children accounted for 33 percent of the city's population. By 1855, they constituted 53 percent. During 1860–1890, the percentage held steady at about 35 percent. By 1880, 56 percent of the foreign-born population was Irish; 8 percent was English; 6 percent was German; 1 percent was Italian; 20 percent hailed from British America; and 3 percent came from elsewhere (ibid., 239; Tables VI, IX, and XXX).

11. Ibid., 74.

12. According to the Boston city directories, there were at least fifty-six eating venues in 1830. By 1860, there were 133, not including hotel restaurants. In 1890, there were 444 restaurants listed in the Boston business directory, an increase of more than 560 percent. See *The Boston Directory Containing Names of the Inhabitants, Occupations, Places of Business, and Dwelling Houses* (Boston: Charles Stimpson, 1830); *The Boston Directory, Embracing the City Record, General Directory of the Citizens, and a Business Directory* (Boston: Adams, Sampson, 1860); *The Boston Directory: Containing the City Record, a Directory of the Citizens, Business Directory, and Street Directory: For the Year Commencing July 1, 1890* (Boston: Sampson, Murdock, 1890).

13. Employed women in antebellum Boston were most likely to find work being domestic servants or doing outwork (taking in washing, ironing, sewing, or mending). In each of these occupations, women's workplaces were private homes (either their own or their employers'), and they could thus eat their meals in the home as well. Virginia Penny, *The Employments of Women: A Cyclopaedia of Woman's Work* (Boston: Walker & Wise, 1863), 350–51; Handlin, *Boston's Immigrants,* 81–82. Women's employment options in Boston continued to diversify throughout the century, though domestic service still employed 44.8 percent of Boston's female wage earners as late as 1880. See Alice Kessler Harris, *Out to Work: A History of Wage-Earning Women in the United States* (New York: Oxford University Press, 1982); Sarah Deutsch, *Women and the City: Gender, Space, and Power in Boston, 1870–1940* (New York: Oxford University Press, 2000); and David M. Katzman, *Seven Days a Week: Women and Domestic Service in Industrializing America* (Urbana: University of Illinois Press, 1981), 287.

14. On the steady expansion of domestic consumption throughout this period, see Richard Bushman, *The Refinement of America: Persons, Houses, Cities* (New York: Vintage, 1993).

15. On the promotion of cultural and intellectual interests in Boston, see Thomas O'Connor, *The Athens of America: Boston, 1825–1840* (Amherst: University of Massachusetts Press, 2006), especially 91–125.

16. On the development of tenements in Boston, see Handlin, *Boston's Immigrants,* 101–14. On boardinghouses, see Wendy Gamber, *The Boardinghouse in Nineteenth-Century America* (Baltimore: Johns Hopkins University Press, 2007).

Notes to Introduction

Boardinghouse proprietors were obligated to provide meals to their residents, but many boarders nevertheless preferred to dine in restaurants. On lodging houses, see Mark Peel, "On the Margins: Lodgers and Boarders in Boston, 1860–1900," *Journal of American History* 72, no. 4 (March 1986): 812–34.

17. Handlin, *Boston's Immigrants*, 63–69, and Table XIII; Stephen Thernstrom, *Poverty and Progress: Social Mobility in a Nineteenth-Century City* (Cambridge, Mass.: Harvard University Press, 1964), Table 4. Peter R. Knights, *The Plain People of Boston, 1830–1860: A Study in City Growth* (New York: Oxford University Press, 1971), 78–102.

18. For example, in the 1850 federal census, 65 percent of employed Irish immigrants in Boston were listed either as laborers or domestic servants. Twenty-eight percent of employed African Americans worked either as laborers or domestic servants; another 25 percent were seamen. In contrast, the occupations held by those of other ethnicities were more diverse. Handlin, *Boston's Immigrants*, Table XIII; Thomas O'Connor, *The Boston Irish: A Political History* (Boston: Northeastern University Press, 1995); Noel Ignatiev, *How the Irish Became White* (New York: Routledge, 1995); James Oliver Horton and Lois E. Horton, *Black Bostonians: Family Life and Community Struggle in the Antebellum North* (New York: Holmes & Meier, 1979).

19. Matthew Frye Jacobson, *Whiteness of a Different Color: European Immigrants and the Alchemy of Race* (Cambridge, Mass.: Harvard University Press, 1998); Elizabeth H. Pleck, *Black Migration and Poverty: Boston, 1865–1900* (New York: Academic Press, 1979).

20. Ted Clarke, *Beacon Hill, Back Bay, and the Building of Boston's Golden Age* (Charleston, S.C.: History Press, 2010); Lawrence Kennedy, *Planning the City upon a Hill: Boston since 1630* (Boston: University of Massachusetts Press, 1992); Walter Muir Whitehill, *Boston: A Topographical History* (Cambridge, Mass.: Belknap, 1968).

21. Sam Bass Warner, *Streetcar Suburbs: The Process of Growth in Boston, 1870–1900* (Cambridge, Mass.: Harvard University Press, 1978); Charles J. Kennedy, "Commuter Services in the Boston Area, 1835–1860," *Business History Review* 36, no. 2 (Summer 1962): 153–70. After the Civil War, Boston aggressively annexed its suburbs, increasing the population and size of the city by 107, 533 people and 20,000 acres. Boston annexed Roxbury in 1867, Dorchester in 1869, and West Roxbury, Brighton, and Charlestown in 1873 (Meckel, "Immigration, Mortality, and Population Growth in Boston," 411).

22. Richard Meckel has found that as a result of landfill projects and suburbanization, the percentage of the population residing south of the city core grew from just 7 percent in 1855 to more than 44 percent in 1880 ("Immigration, Mortality, and Population Growth in Boston," 410).

23. C. Pinney, *Atlas of the City of Boston* (Boston: L. Prang, 1861), Plate 23.

24. Horton and Horton, *Black Bostonians*, 3.

25. Frederick A. Bushee, *Ethnic Factors in the Population of Boston* (1903; reprint, New York: Arno Press, 1970), 26; Dwight Porter, *Report upon a Sanitary Inspection*

of Certain Tenement-House Districts of Boston (Boston: Press of Rockwell and Churchill, 1889), 7.

26. The rich literature considering nineteenth-century American foodways and the window that diet and dining provide into American society and culture includes Kenneth L. Ames, *Death in the Dining Room and Other Tales of Victorian Culture* (Philadelphia: Temple University Press, 1992); Abigail Carroll, *Three Squares: The Invention of the American Meal* (New York: Basic Books, 2013); Barbara Carson, *Ambitious Appetites: Dining, Behavior, and Patterns of Consumption in Federal Washington* (Washington, D.C.: American Institute of Architects Press, 1990); Hasia Diner, *Hungering for America: Italian, Irish, and Jewish Foodways in the Age of Migration* (Cambridge, Mass.: Harvard University Press, 2001); Donna R. Gabaccia, *We Are What We Eat: Food and the Making of Americans* (Cambridge, Mass.: Harvard University Press, 1998); Kathryn Grover, ed., *Dining in America, 1850–1900* (Amherst: University of Massachusetts Press and the Margret Woodbury Strong Museum, 1987); Andrew P. Haley, *Turning the Tables: American Restaurant Culture and the Rise of the Middle Class, 1880–1920* (Chapel Hill: University of North Carolina Press, 2011); Kristin L. Hoganson, *Consumers' Imperium: The Global Production of American Domesticity, 1865–1920* (Chapel Hill: University of North Carolina Press, 2007); John F. Kasson, *Rudeness & Civility: Manners in Nineteenth-Century Urban America* (New York: Hill & Wang, 1990); Harvey Levenstein, *Paradox of Plenty: A Social History of Eating in Modern America* (New York: Oxford University Press, 1993) and *Revolution at the Table: The Transformation of the American Diet* (New York: Oxford University Press, 1988); Michael Lesy and Lisa Stoffer, *Repast: Dining Out at the Dawn of the New American Century, 1900–1910* (New York: W. W. Norton, 2013); Cindy Lobel, *Urban Appetites: Food and Culture in Nineteenth-Century New York* (Chicago: University of Chicago Press, 2014); John F. Mariani, *America Eats Out: An Illustrated History of Restaurants, Taverns, Coffee Shops, Speakeasies, and Other Establishments That Have Fed Us for 350 Years* (New York: Morrow, 1991); James E. McWilliams, *A Revolution in Eating: How the Quest for Food Shaped America* (New York: Columbia University Press, 2005); Sandra Oliver, *Saltwater Foodways: New Englanders and Their Food at Sea and Ashore in the Nineteenth Century* (Mystic, Conn.: Mystic Seaport Museum, 1995); Richard Pillsbury, *From Boarding House to Bistro: The American Restaurant Then and Now* (Boston: Unwin Hyman, 1990); Laura Shapiro, *Perfection Salad: Women and Cooking at the Turn of the Century* (New York: Farrar, Straus and Giroux, 1986); Jessica Ellen Sewell, *Women and the Everyday City: Public Spaces in San Francisco, 1890–1915* (Minneapolis: University of Minnesota Press, 2011); Katherine Leonard Turner, *How the Other Half Ate: A History of Working-Class Meals at the Turn of the Century* (Berkeley: University of California Press, 2014); Susan Williams, *Savory Suppers and Fashionable Feasts: Dining in Victorian America* (New York: Pantheon, 1985); Jan Whitaker, *Tea at the Blue Lantern Inn: A Social History of the Tea Room Craze in America* (New York: St. Martin's Press, 2002); Jane Ziegelman, *97 Orchard: An Edible History of Five Immigrant Families in One New York Tenement* (New York:

Smithsonian Books, 2010). Of these authors, only Gabaccia, Haley, Lesy and Stoffer, Lobel, Mariani, and Pillsbury seriously consider restaurant dining. There is also an emphasis on the second half of the century among these works, with the exception of Lobel, McWilliams, and Carson.

27. Mary Ryan, *Civic Wars: Democracy and Public Life in the American City during the Nineteenth Century* (Berkeley: University of California Press, 1998).

28. David Waldstreicher, *In the Midst of Perpetual Fetes: The Making of American Nationalism, 1776–1820* (Chapel Hill: University of North Carolina Press, 1997); Ryan, *Civic Wars.*

29. In contrast to Richard Bushman, who has found that growing consumption in the nineteenth century helped to obscure class differences in America, I find that Bostonians used the key vehicle of commercial dining and the arena of the restaurant in part to express and reinforce differences between them (Bushman, *The Refinement of America,* 404).

30. The nineteenth century is generally understood by historians to have been a period of steadily intensifying segregation and conflict between urbanites of different socioeconomic, ethnic, and racial groups. See, for example, Leonard Curry, *The Free Black in Urban America, 1800–1850: The Shadow of a Dream* (Chicago: University of Chicago Press, 1981); Jacobson, *Whiteness of a Different Color; James Oliver Horton, Black Bostonians: Family Life and Community Struggle in the Antebellum North* (New York: Holmes and Meier, 1979); Lobel, *Urban Appetites;* David Roediger, *The Wages of Whiteness: Race and the Making of the American Working Class* (London: Verso, 2007); Ryan, *Civic Wars;* and Waldstreicher, *In the Midst of Perpetual Fetes.*

31. Samantha Barbas, "'I'll Take Chop Suey': Restaurants as Agents of Culinary and Cultural Change," *Journal of Popular Culture* 36, no. 4 (May 2003): 683.

32. Charles Sellers, *The Market Revolution: Jacksonian America, 1815–1846* (New York: Oxford University Press, 1994).

33. William Grimes *Appetite City: A Culinary History of New York* (New York: North Point Press, 2010); Haley, *Turning the Tables,* 14.

34. Thomas O'Connor, *The Athens of America: Boston, 1825–1840* (Amherst: University of Massachusetts Press, 2006); Paul Goodman, "Ethics and Enterprise: The Values of a Boston Elite, 1800–1860," *American Quarterly* 18, no. 3 (1966): 437–51; Frederic Cople Jaher, *The Urban Establishment: Upper Strata in Boston, New York, Charleston, Chicago, and Los Angeles* (Urbana: University of Illinois Press, 1982).

35. Stephen Nissenbaum, *Sex, Diet, and Debility in Jacksonian America: Sylvester Graham and Health Reform* (Westport, Conn.: Greenwood Press, 1980).

36. Cindy Lobel, "Sylvester Graham and Antebellum Diet Reform," *History Now.* https://www.gilderlehrman.org/history-by-era/first-age-reform/essays/sylvester-graham-and-antebellum-diet-reform [accessed February 9, 2016].

37. Harvey Levenstein, "The New England Kitchen and the Origins of Modern American Eating Habits," *American Quarterly* 32, no. 4 (Autumn 1980): 369–86; Shapiro, *Perfection Salad,* 48, 148.

Notes to Chapter 1

1. FILET DE BOEUF AT THE TREMONT HOUSE

1. This dinner was reported by several Boston newspapers including the *Boston Weekly Messenger,* October 22, 1829; *Boston Daily Advertiser,* October 19, 1829; *Boston Commercial Gazette,* October 19, 1829; and *Boston Courier,* October 19, 1829. Quotes from the *Weekly Messenger.*

2. Molly Winger Berger, "The Modern Hotel in America, 1829–1929" (Ph.D. diss.: Case Western University, 1997), 71.

3. Sharon Salinger, *Taverns and Drinking in Early America* (Baltimore: Johns Hopkins University Press, 2004).

4. Samuel Adams Drake, *Old Boston Taverns and Tavern Clubs* (Boston: W. A. Butterfield, 1917).

5. The *Yankee,* May 28, 1813.

6. McWilliams, *A Revolution in Eating,* 260–63. Sharon Salinger, in *Taverns and Drinking in Early America* argues that early American taverns were less democratic than McWilliams suggests. In any case, she agrees they became steadily more stratified over time.

7. Richard Bushman, *The Refinement of America,* 160–64. In French, *hôtel* referred to the city homes of the French nobility.

8. Jefferson Williamson, *The American Hotel: An Anecdotal History* (1930; reprint, New York: Arno Press, 1970), 195.

9. On influences in early American cooking, see Waverly Root and Richard de Rochemont, *Eating in America: A History* (New York: Ecco Press, 1976); and McWilliams, *A Revolution in Eating.*

10. Williamson, *The American Hotel,* 194.

11. John F. D. Smyth, *Tour in the United States of America . . .* (1784; reprint, 2 vols., New York: New York Times, 1968), 1:49.

12. The creation of a restaurant culture was already under way before the French Revolution, but the Revolution certainly accelerated it. Stephen Mennell, *All Manners of Food,* 138–39; Rebecca Spang, *The Invention of the Restaurant: Paris and Modern Gastronomic Culture* (Cambridge, Mass.: Harvard University Press, 2000), 9–11. Interestingly, in French hotels that catered to Americans, the table d'hôte system lingered.

13. "Old-Time Caterers," *Boston Daily Globe,* February 14, 1887, 2.

14. Andrew F. Smith, ed., "Julien's Restorator," in *The Oxford Companion to American Food and Drink* (New York: Oxford University Press, 2007), 550; James Henry Stark, *Antique Views of Ye Towne of Boston* (Boston: Photo-Electrotype Engraving, 1882), 75. Mr. Julien received the most attention from his fellow Frenchmen. In particular, he won the praise of famed gastronome and creator of the food essay genre Jean Anthelme Brillat-Savarin. Today, Julien's is remembered as the first restaurant in America.

15. *Boston Price Current and Marine Intelligencer,* August 7, 1797.

16. *Boston Daily Advertiser,* June 11, 1828.

Notes to Chapter 1   121

17. Justin Winsor, *The Memorial History of the City of Boston* . . . (4 vols., Boston: Ticknor, 1881–1883), 4:55; Doris Elizabeth King, "The First Class Hotel and the Age of the Common Man," *Journal of Southern History* 23, no. 2 (May 1957): 178–79.

18. On the early development of American foodways and regional differences, see McWilliams, *Revolution in Eating.*

19. J. E. Alexander, *Transatlantic Sketches* (2 vols., London: Richard Bentley, 1822), 2:102.

20. Carson, *Ambitious Appetites,* 68.

21. Englishwoman Frances Trollope discusses how infrequently laundry was done in the American hotels she visited. Trollope, *Domestic Manners of the Americans* (1832; reprint, New York: Vintage, 1960), 1:276.

22. Margaret Hall quoted in Jack Larkin, *The Reshaping of Everyday Life, 1790–1840* (New York: Harper Perennial, 1988), 181.

23. Hall quoted in Carson, *Ambitious Appetites,* 61.

24. For example, see Trollope, *Domestic Manners of the Americans.*

25. Webster quoted in Eric Slaughter, *The State as a Work of Art: The Cultural Origins of the Constitution* (Chicago: University of Chicago Press, 2009), 71.

26. Gordon Wood, *The American Revolution, a History* (New York: Modern Library, 2002).

27. Quoted in McWilliams, *A Revolution in Eating,* 303.

28. Webster quoted in ibid., 301.

29. Quoted in Carson, *Ambitious Appetites,* 70

30. O'Connor, *The Athens of America,* 129.

31. This dilemma was similar to the one Americans faced regarding how to dress themselves. Kate Haulman, *The Politics of Fashion in Eighteenth-Century America* (Chapel Hill: University of North Carolina Press, 2011), 175.

32. McWilliams, *A Revolution in Eating,* 302. Such sentiments were echoed in other cultural realms, including fashion. See Haulman, *The Politics of Fashion,* 220.

33. O'Connor, *The Athens of America.*

34. Peter Dobkin Hall, *The Organization of American Culture, 1700–1900: Private Institutions, Elites, and the Origins of American Nationality* (New York: New York University Press, 1982); Paul Goodman, "Ethics and Enterprise: The Values of a Boston Elite, 1800–1860," *American Quarterly* 18, no. 3 (1966): 437–51; Frederic Cople Jaher, *The Urban Establishment: Upper Strata in Boston, New York, Charleston, Chicago, and Los Angeles* (Urbana: University of Illinois Press, 1982).

35. Goodman, "Ethics and Enterprise."

36. Steven Watts has argued that the War of 1812 marked a watershed in the transition from classical republicanism to liberalism. Watts, *The Republic Reborn: War and the Making of Liberal America, 1790–1820* (Baltimore: Johns Hopkins University Press, 1987), 11.

37. Bushman, *The Refinement of America.*

38. Ibid.

39. The ideology of refinement dovetailed with what French sociologist Pierre Bourdieu has called "cultural capital," or expertise in cultural matters like dining etiquette. Bourdieu argues that the expenditure of cultural capital is as effective in differentiating and legitimizing class distinctions as the outlay of actual capital. Pierre Bourdieu, *Distinction: A Social Critique of the Judgment of Taste* (Cambridge, Mass.: Cambridge University Press, 1984), 66.

40. As historians of consumption have argued, the changes outlined here should be understood as a continuation of a trend that had begun at least by the seventeenth century. See, for example, T. H. Breen, *The Marketplace of Revolution: How Consumer Politics Shaped American Independence* (New York: Oxford University Press, 2005). However, in the early nineteenth century, the changes quickened in pace.

41. On the changing production of tableware, see Carson, *Ambitious Appetites*, 68–70. On the increasing specialization of forks see John Kasson, *Rudeness and Civility: Manners in Nineteenth-Century Urban America* (New York: Hill & Wang, 1990), 189.

42. Bushman, *The Refinement of America*.

43. Kasson, *Rudeness and Civility*; Karen Halttunen, *Confidence Men and Painted Women: A Study of Middle-class Culture in America, 1830–1870* (New Haven, Conn.: Yale University Press, 1982).

44. Nathaniel Dearborn, *Dearborn's Reminiscences of Boston and Guide through the City and Environs* (Boston: Nathaniel Dearborn, 1841), 142.

45. Quoted in William Harvard Eliot, *A Description of the Tremont House with Architectural Illustrations* (Boston: Gray & Bowen, 1830), 1. In 1825, the Boston newspaper the *American Traveler* reported on the "astonishing revolution . . . wrought to all modes of traveling" and the remarkable increase in travelers that had resulted (*American Traveler,* July 8, 1825).

46. *Boston Newsletter and Public Record,* April 29, 1826.

47. A letter from Eliot's son, Dr. Samuel Eliot, to the Bostonian Society to commemorate the Tremont upon the building's destruction in 1895, stated that his father had developed a style of hotel "entirely new, not only in this country, but in Europe." Quoted in Berger, *The Modern Hotel in America,* 49.

48. Ibid., 41–43.

49. Berger provides a more thorough account of the Tremont's innovations in "The Modern Hotel in America," 63–69. She explains that the total cost was high because the Tremont used expensive building materials, like granite, and elaborate decorations. It also incorporated sophisticated technology throughout. In comparison, a similarly sized, more traditional hotel in New York cost $130,000 (ibid., 34–35).

50. Henry Lee, "Boston's Greatest Hotel," *Old Time New England* 55, no. 200 (Spring 1965): 99.

Notes to Chapter 1

51. Charles Augustus Murray, *Travels in North America during the Years 1834, 1835, & 1836 . . .*, 2 vols. (London: Richard Bentley, 1839), 1:102; James Boardman, *America and the Americans* (London: Longman, Reese, Orme, Brown, Green, & Longman, 1833), 280–81.

52. Godfrey T. Vigne, *Six Months in America* (Philadelphia: Thomas T. Ash, 1833), 104; Charles Dickens, *American Notes for General Circulation and Pictures from Italy* (London: Chapman and Hall, 1913), 21; *Gleason's Pictorial* 2 (February 7, 1852): 88.

53. Eliot, *A Description of the Tremont House.*

54. Abel Bowen, *Bowen's Picture of Boston, or the Citizen's and Stranger's Guide to the Metropolis of Massachusetts and Its Environs* (Boston: Abel Bowen, 1829), 20.

55. Berger, "The Modern Hotel in America," 56.

56. Eliot, *A Description of the Tremont House*, 11.

57. Williamson, *The American Hotel*, 15.

58. Eliot, *A Description of the Tremont House*, 11. On light in the practice of refinement, see Bushman, *The Refinement of America*, 127. The Tremont was not the first hotel to have gaslight, but the technology was still considered novel when the hotel opened.

59. Eliot, *A Description of the Tremont House*, 11.

60. Lee, "Boston's Greatest Hotel," 100.

61. Dickens, *American Notes*, 51.

62. Eliza Leslie, *Miss Leslie's Behavior Book, a Guide and Manual for Ladies* (Philadelphia: T. B. Peterson and Brothers, 1859), 104.

63. Mary Caroline Crawford, *Romantic Days in Old Boston: The Story of the City and of Its People during the Nineteenth Century* (Boston: Little, Brown, 1910), 347–48.

64. Sly, *Sayings and Doings at the Tremont*, 1:9.

65. Tunis Gulic Campbell outlines the procedure for hotel waiters in *Hotel Keepers, Head Waiters, and Housekeepers' Guide* (Boston: Coolidge and Wiley, 1848), 13–19.

66. The terms *bill of fare* and *menu* were generally used interchangeably. But according to at least one well-regarded source, there was a distinction between them: as the famous caterer Jessup Whitehead explained, "The menu is the fare, the bill of fare is to tell what the fare consists of . . . , as if one should say, 'this is my library; this is the catalogue of my library.'" Whitehead, *The Steward's Handbook and Dictionary* (Chicago: J. Anderson, 1889), 47.

67. Sly, *Sayings and Doings at the Tremont*, 1:139.

68. This practice is evident in several of the Boston menus housed by the American Antiquarian Society.

69. Lee, "Boston's Greatest Hotel," 101.

70. McWilliams, *A Revolution in Eating*, 309.

71. James Trager, *The Food Chronology: A Food Lovers' Compendium of Events and Anecdotes from Prehistory to the Present* (New York: Henry Holt, 1995), 195.

72. On the development of French cuisine and the French culinary profession, see Stephen Mennell, *All Manners of Food*; Priscilla Parkhurst Ferguson, "A Cultural Field in the Making: Gastronomy in Nineteenth-Century France," in *French Food: On the Table, On the Page, and in French Culture*, ed. Lawrence R. Schehr and Allen S. Weiss (New York: Routledge, 2001), 26–31; and Amy B. Trubek, *Haute Cuisine: How the French Invented the Culinary Profession* (Philadelphia: University of Pennsylvania Press, 2000).

73. *State Street: A Brief Account of a Boston Way* (Boston: State Street Trust Company, 1906), 18.

74. See the menu, "Public Dinner, Given at the Exchange Coffee House . . . In Honor of General La Fayette," Exchange Coffee House, Boston, August 24, 1824; collection of the American Antiquarian Society, Boston.

75. Haley, *Turning the Tables*, 32.

76. See discussion of kitchen staff later in this chapter.

77. Menu, "The Tremont House," Boston, April 7, 1839; collection of the American Antiquarian Society, Boston.

78. Menu, "The Tremont House," Boston, June 16, 1843; collection of the American Antiquarian Society, Boston.

79. Charles H. Wiggin, *Diary for 1859–1860*; collection of the American Antiquarian Society, Boston, June 26, 1859.

80. William Toynbee, *The Diaries of William Charles MacReady, 1833–1851*, 2 vols. (New York: G. P. Putnam, 1912), 2:224.

81. *The Letters and Journals of General Nicholas Longworth Anderson*, ed. Isabel Anderson (New York: Fleming Revell, 1942), 31; Williamson, *The American Hotel*, 14.

82. [Eliza War Farrar], *The Young Lady's Friend* (Boston: American Stationers' Co., 1837), 346–47.

83. Americans did develop the unique habit of "zigzagging" when eating with a knife and fork, whereby they transferred the fork from left to right after cutting a piece of food with the knife and then raising the food to their mouth using the fork, now in the left hand. This process is described in Leslie, *Miss Leslie's Behavior Book*, 127.

84. Eliza Leslie makes this argument in *Domestic French Cookery* (Philadelphia: Carey & Hart, 1832).

85. Lydia Marie Child, *The American Frugal Housewife, Dedicated to Those Who Are Not Ashamed of Economy*, 12th ed. (Boston: Carter, Hendee, 1832; reprint, Worthington, Ohio: Worthington Historical Society, 1965), 99. Quoted in Berger, "The Modern Hotel in America," 29.

86. Bushman, *The Refinement of America*, 411.

87. Berger makes this point in "The Modern Hotel in America," 53.

88. See, for example, *Boston Commercial Gazette*, July 7, 1828.

89. Franklin quoted in Berger, "The Modern Hotel in America," 32.

Notes to Chapter 1 125

90. The description "palace of the public" was first coined by the *American Intelligencer* in 1827 (Berger, "The Modern Hotel in America," 85). See also King, "The First Class Hotel and the Age of the Common Man," especially 185.

91. *Boston Courier,* October 22, 1829.

92. Berger, "The Modern Hotel in America," 71.

93. Lee, "Boston's Greatest Hotel," 101. "Dining Considered as a Fine Art," *Harper's New Monthly Magazine* 18, no. 103 (December 1858), 68. French refugee Pierre Blot opened America's first culinary school in New York City in 1865. In 1866, "Professor" Blot came to Boston and offered a month-long course at Mercantile Hall. The lessons Blot gave in Boston were later compiled and published in a book titled *Prof. Blot's Lectures on Cookery, Delivered at Mercantile Hall* (n.p., 1866). Jan Longone, "Professor Blot and the First French Cooking School in New York, Part I," *Gastronomica* 1, no. 2 (May 2001): 65–71.

94. Seventh Census of the United States, 1850, Manuscript Population schedules, Boston City, Suffolk County, Massachusetts.

95. *Acton in America: The American Journal of Sir John Acton, 1853,* ed. Sydney Jackman (Shepherdstown, W.Va.: Patmos Press, 1979), 48.

96. For example, see E. T. Coke, *A Subaltern's Furlough: Descriptive Scenes in Various Parts of the United States, Upper and Lower Canada, New Brunswick and Nova Scotia, during the Summer and Autumn of 1832,* 2 vols. (New York: J. & J. Harper, 1833), 1:32; and *Acton in America,* 48. Both writers attribute the unwillingness of white, native-born Americans to perform these jobs to the servility associated with them.

97. For some descriptions of working conditions later in the century, see for example Eliot, *A Description of the Tremont House; Boston Daily Globe,* February 3, 1878; February 24, 1878; and August 7, 1885.

98. I have been unable to find reports of chefs' earnings in Boston before the Civil War. But the *Galaxy* reported in 1867 that most chefs earned between $60 and $200 per month. Pierre Blot, "Modern and Mediaeval Dinners," *Galaxy* 3, no. 7 (April 1867): 723. The *Boston Investigator* reported in 1872 that the chef at the Parker House was paid $4,000 a year (*Boston Investigator,* March 19, 1879).

99. *Boston Daily Globe,* August 7, 1885. Seventh Census of the United States, 1850, Manuscript population schedules, Boston City, Suffolk County, Massachusetts.

100. To get a sense of retention rates for nineteenth-century cooks, I consulted *City Directories* for Boston, tracking men listed as cooks. (Women listed in the occupation likely worked in private households.) The number of male cooks still employed in the occupation after five years was negligible throughout the century.

101. Campbell describes the typical waiter's dress in *Hotel Keepers, Head Waiters, and Housekeepers' Guide,* 31–33.

102. Many antebellum menus included a request that patrons not "fee" the waiters. For example, Menu, "Parker House Bill of Fare," the Parker House, Boston, January 15, 1856, American Antiquarian Society collection. Tunis Campbell

advised against tipping waiters in his advice book *Hotel Keepers, Head Waiters, and Housekeepers' Guide*, 8–9. Frances Wright first noticed Americans' ban on tipping waiters in 1821. She attributed the cause to "the republican habits and feelings of the community," adding, "I honor the pride which makes a man unwilling to sell his personal service to a fellow creature." Wright, *Views of Society and Manners in America*, ed. Paul R. Baker (1821: reprint, Cambridge, Mass.: Belknap Press, 1963), 119. This prohibition against tipping, however, did not last. In the decades after the Civil War, tips became extremely useful for securing special treatment at restaurants, a central component of the conspicuous consumption of the Gilded Age.

103. Royall Tyler, *The Contrast: A Comedy in Five Acts* (Boston: Houghton Mifflin, 1920), 54.

104. Campbell, *Hotel Keepers, Head Waiters, and Housekeepers' Guide*, 11.

105. Philip S. Foner and Ronald L. Lewis, eds., *The Black Worker: A Documentary History from Colonial Times to the Present*, 2 vols. (Philadelphia: Temple University Press, 1978), 1:191–99.

106. For a full account of Minkins's story, see Gary Collison, *Shadrach Minkins: From Fugitive Slave to Citizen* (Cambridge, Mass.: Harvard University Press, 1997).

107. For accounts of the arrest, see the *National Anti-Slavery Standard*, February 20, 1851; *Boston Daily Evening Transcript*, February 9, 1886; and other Boston newspapers. See also Collison, *Shadrach Minkins*, 112–13.

108. Collison, *Shadrach Minkins*, chapter 9.

109. Bushman, *The Refinement of America*, 406.

110. Important political and diplomatic figures feted at the Tremont included Presidents Andrew Jackson and John Tyler; Gustave de Beaumont; Alexis de Tocqueville; Prince de Joinville, the son of Louis Philippe; and Lord Ashburton.

111. James Boardman, *America and the Americans* (London: Longman, Rees, Orme, Brown, Green, and Longman, 1833), 26.

112. Ibid., 186–87.

113. Tudor, *Diary of a Tour in North America*, 37–38.

114. For a gendered reading of the entire hotel environment, see Molly Winger Berger, "A House Divided: Technology, Gender, and Consumption in America's Luxury Hotels, 1825–1860," in *His and Hers: Gender, Consumption, and Technology*, ed. Roger Horowitz and Arwen Mohun (Charlottesville: University Press of Virginia, 1997), 39–65.

115. Isaiah Rogers himself would be commissioned to design many of the Tremont's imitators, including the Astor House (New York City, 1836); Burnet House (Cincinnati, 1849–50); St. Charles (New Orleans, 1837); Battle House (Mobile, Alabama, 1852–53); Maxwell House—yes, that Maxwell House—(Nashville, 1862–65); and the Galt House (Louisville, 1865). As a result, Rogers would become known as the "father of the modern hotel." Additional luxury hotels throughout the country included New York's Fifth Avenue Hotel (1859); Philadelphia's American House (1845), Lafayette (1853), and Continental (1860); and New Orleans's St. Louis (1831; rebuilt in 1841).

Notes to Chapter 1   127

116. Lee, "Boston's Greatest Hotel," 104; John Phoenix [Captain George H. Derby], *The Squibbob Papers* (New York: Carleton, 1865), 139.

117. William Grimes, *Appetite City*, 48–49. For the full Delmonico's story, see Lately Thomas, *Delmonico's: A Century of Splendor* (New York: Houghton Mifflin, 1967). Delmonico's opened as a freestanding, full-service French restaurant in 1831 but initially boasted none of the physical grandeur of the Tremont House. After a fire devastated its original building in 1835, Delmonico's rebuilt its restaurant in a much more prestigious structure and quickly catapulted to the pinnacle of luxury dining in America.

118. James W. Spring, *Boston and the Parker House: A Chronicle of Those Who Have Lived on That Historic Spot Where the New Parker House Now Stands in Boston* (Boston: J. R. Whipple, 1927), 141.

119. *Boston Courier,* June 15, 1843.

120. Spring, *Boston and the Parker House,* 141. Louis Ober of the famed Ober's Restaurant Parisian Café, later Locke-Ober Restaurant, got his start much the same way as Parker. He began in a small cellar café in the 1850s on Winter Place, slowly establishing a reputation for himself and upgraded his business to become a fine dining Boston institution that continues to exist today.

121. Spring, *Boston and the Parker House,* 141.

122. Thorstein Veblen, *The Theory of the Leisure Class: An Economic Study of Institutions* (New York: Modern Library, 1934), 68–75.

123. On the full development of what historian Andrew Haley calls the "aristocratic" American restaurant experience, see *Turning the Tables,* 19–41. The longtime conservatism of Boston's elite held Bostonians back from embracing the highest levels of luxury exhibited in New York. But Bostonians still utilized the refined public dining experience—choosing the right venue, securing the right table, wearing the right clothes, and exhibiting standards of good taste—in their effort to secure membership among the privileged and powerful members of Boston society.

124. Lawrence Levine, *Highbrow Lowbrow: The Emergence of Cultural Hierarchy in America* (Cambridge, Mass.: Harvard University Press, 1988), 146.

125. Haley, *Turning the Tables,* 23–33.

126. "Ways of a Hotel Waiter," *Boston Daily Advertiser,* September 25, 1888, 2.

127. "Hotel Waiters' Fees," *Boston Daily Globe,* February 9, 1884, 8.

128. *Boston Daily Advertiser,* December 6, 1886, 4.

129. See, for example, Leslie, *Miss Leslie's Behavior Book,* 120–23.

130. On the elaboration of table manners in the nineteenth century, see Kasson, *Rudeness and Civility,* 182–214. Etiquette manual quoted in ibid., 204.

131. *How to Behave: A Pocket Manual of Republican Etiquette and Guide to Correct Personal Habits* (New York: Samuel R. Wells, 1872), 83–84.

132. Thomas Walker, *The Art of Dining and the Art of Attaining Health, with a Few Hints on Suppers* (Philadelphia: E. L Carey & A. Hart, 1837), 60.

133. Wiggin, *Diary*, July 27, 1859 entry. In fact, Wiggin did finally get to dine at Parker's about a year later. "Mr. Wilson," an older family friend, treated the boy after Wiggin repeatedly suggested it. Wiggin described the meal as "tip-top." He especially liked the warm headcheese. Wiggin, *Diary*, March 21, 1860 entry.

134. Wiggin, *Diary*, March 21, 1860 entry.

135. Quoted in Lee, "Boston's Greatest Hotel," 104.

2. BOLTED BEEF AND BOLTED PUDDING

1. "Journeymen Ship Carpenters and Caulkers of Boston," *New England Artisan*, June 21, 1832, 1. Thanks to Christopher Sawula for alerting me to this source.

2. John R. Gillis, *A World of Their Own Making: Myth, Ritual, and the Quest for Family Values* (New York: Basic Books, 1996), 90–94.

3. "Why We Get Sick," *Harper's New Monthly Magazine* 13, no. 77 (October 1856): 642.

4. Cindy Lobel finds that a very similar process occurred in New York City during this period. *Urban Appetites,*106, 112–15.

5. Female eating house proprietors in nineteenth-century Boston were rare, but they did exist. Unfortunately, their numbers are impossible to determine. Census takers did not record occupational information for women until 1870. Likewise, city directories recorded occupational information only for heads of household, typically men. Meanwhile, business directories often listed only the initials of proprietors, making it impossible to determine whether the person was male or female. Nevertheless, seven female names do appear in the 1850 federal census as restaurant proprietors. What specific genre of venue they operated (or why their names made it into the census) is not known. Another clue about female proprietorship is provided by the Married Women Doing Business Certificates, a collection available at the Boston City Archives. Between 1862 and 1974, Chapter 209 of the Massachusetts General Laws required any married women doing business on her own account to record in the City Clerk's Office a certificate stating her name and the name of her husband, as well as the nature and location of her business. The surviving certificates show that between 1862 and 1891, there were thirteen married women who recorded their business as an "eating house" (Married Women Doing Business Certificates, vols. 1–6, Boston City Archives, Boston). It is likely that many women married to eating house proprietors also assisted in the business and thus would have been present in the venue.

6. Daniel E. Sutherland, *Americans and Their Servants: Domestic Service in the United States from 1800 to 1920* (Baton Rouge: Louisiana State University Press, 1981), 113.

7. Mixed-gender cafés, where women of all classes could dine alone, with other women, or with their beaus, husbands, or families, expanded considerably later in the century. (This will be the subject of chapter 4.) Still, women tended to avoid the male-dominated eating house.

Notes to Chapter 2   129

8. The *Boston Daily Globe* reminisced about the city's early eating house trade in "Congress Street: Once a Place for Epicurean Enjoyment," June 2, 1889, 8.

9. In 1832, the mayor and city aldermen voted to extend liquor licensing to those businesses that sold food to be consumed on the premises. Prior to this, a business owner had to demonstrate he provided both board and rooms if he wanted a liquor license. Even after the relaxation of requirements, the liquor licensing laws were widely violated throughout the century. City Document 140, 1868, "List of Names of Parties Who Sell or Keep Intoxicating Liquors." The list was compiled by John Kurtz, chief of police. See also the 1867 license debates: *Reports on the Subject of a License Law*, Mass. House Doc. 415, 1867, especially the appendix; Theodore Voelckers, *Suggestions for a Law to Regulate the Sale of Spiritous and Malt Liquors* (Boston: Rockwell & Vollins, 1867), 1–10.

10. According to the *Boston Directory*, approximately 85 percent of restaurant keepers in 1830 had the same business address as their home address. For 1840, this figure was 95 percent; 77 percent in 1850; and 71 percent in 1860. In making these calculations, I assumed that those residents who listed only a business address or only a home address instead of two different addresses lived and worked in the same building. This is not an outlandish assumption, but it is unconfirmed. *The Boston Directory Containing Names of the Inhabitants, Occupations, Places of Business, and Dwelling Houses* (Boston: Charles Stimpson, 1930); *The Boston Directory Containing Names of the Inhabitants, Occupations, Places of Business, and Dwelling Houses* (Boston: Charles Stimpson, 1840); *The Boston Directory Containing Names of the Inhabitants, Occupations, Places of Business, and Dwelling Houses* (Boston: George Adams, 1850); *The Boston Directory: Embracing the City Record, a General Directory of the Citizens, and a Business Directory* (Boston: Adams, Sampson, 1860).

11. Richard Pillsbury, *From Boardinghouse to Bistro*, 28.

12. These common marketing techniques, which applied earlier in the century as well, are described in "All Around the Hub," *Boston Daily Globe*, February 24, 1878, 2; "Dinner for a Dime," *Boston Daily Globe*, December 24, 1885, 4.

13. "Congress Street," 8; "All Around the Hub," 2.

14. "Why We Get Sick," 642; "Congress Street," 8

15. See, for example, Basil Hall, *Travels in North America in the Years 1827 and 1828* (Edinburgh: Cadell, 1829), 32–34. See also "Why We Get Sick," 645.

16. "Dinner for a Dime," 4.

17. For example, see "The New Ethics of Eating," *Boston Courier*, October 26, 1837, 1; Stephen Nissenbaum, *Sex, Diet, and Debility in Jacksonian America*, 43. Of course, some diet reformers urged Americans to stay away from meat. See ibid., 39–52.

18. Haley, *Turning the Tables*, 141–42.

19. "Congress Street," 8.

20. C. W. Gesner, "Concerning Restaurants," *Harper's New Monthly Magazine* 32, no. 191 (April 1866): 592. See also George Thompson, *Venus in Boston and Other Tales of Nineteenth-century Life*, ed. David S. Reynolds and Kimberly R. Gladman

(Boston: University of Massachusetts Press, 2002), 4; *Boston Daily Globe,* February 24, 1878. George Foster describes a similar phenomenon among the eating houses of New York in his 1856 *New York by Gas-light and Other Urban Sketches,* ed. Stuart Blumin (reprint) (Berkeley: University of California Press, 1990), 216–17.

21. Lobel, *Urban Appetites,* 112–13.

22. Handlin *Boston's Immigrants,* 92–93.

23. John Eaton Whiting, *A Schedule of the Buildings and Their Occupancy, on the Principal Streets and Wharves in the City of Boston* (Boston: Press of W. L. Deland, 1877).

24. Thompson, *Venus in Boston,* 4.

25. "Sayings and Doings in Boston," *Spirit of the Times; A Chronicle of the Turf, Agriculture, Field Sports, Literature, and the Stage* 13 (January 27, 1844): 576.

26. Ibid.

27. In an article in 1887, the *Boston Daily Globe* looked back at restaurants in the 1830s. See "Old Time Caterers," *Boston Daily Globe,* February 14, 1887, 2.

28. "Boston's Working Women—About the Women Who Work in Restaurants," *Boston Globe,* January 13, 1883, 1. This article compared the wages of men and women waiters in eating houses. Female waiters will be discussed in chapter 4.

29. "Dinner for a Dime," 4.

30. "Affairs about Home," *Boston Herald,* April 10, 1857, 4.

31. "Police Court," *Boston Daily Atlas,* October 13, 1854, 2. See also the *Boston Daily Atlas,* January 8, 1849, 2.

32. Seventh Census of the United States, 1850, Manuscript Population schedules, Boston City, Suffolk County, Massachusetts.

33. Untitled article, *National Police Gazette (1845–1906),* June 19, 1847, 325.

34. *Ballou's Dollar Monthly Magazine* 3 (May 1856): 416.

35. "Restaurant Calls," *Boston Daily Globe,* March 25, 1884, 9; "Restaurant Calls," *Boston Daily Globe,* July 10, 1887, 9; "Slang in Restaurants," *Boston Daily Globe,* February 24, 1889, 18.

36. *Hash house* became another name for a cheap eating establishment that catered to working men. Jessica Ellen Sewell, *Women and the Everyday City: Public Spaces in San Francisco, 1890–1915* (Minneapolis: University of Minnesota Press, 2011), 77.

37. Menu quoted in Jan Whitaker, "Prices," Restaurant-ing through History, http://restaurant-ingthroughhistory.com/restaurant-prices/(accessed February 9, 2016).

38. "What Food Costs," *Boston Daily Globe,* May 1, 1887, 20; "Restaurant Costs," *Boston Daily Globe,* June 26, 1887, 18.

39. "A Fifteen-Cent Dinner," *Boston Daily Globe,* December 11, 1883, 6; "Dinner for a Dime," 4.

40. "A Fifteen-Cent Dinner," 6.

41. "Eating House Remodeled," *Boston Daily Advertiser,* June 5, 1850, 2.

42. "All Around the Hub," 2.

Notes to Chapter 2   131

43. As described in Wolfe, *The Lodging House Problem,* 50; "His Luncheon and Hers," *Boston Daily Globe,* January 7, 1894, 16. Whether the napkin rack existed earlier in the century is unclear but seems likely.

44. For example, *Harper's New Monthly Magazine* explained the hierarchy of eating houses by noting differences in style and service between venues but not distinctions in fare. "Concerning Restaurants," 592.

45. "Sayings and Doings in Boston," 576.

46. On the concept of cultural capital, see Pierre Bourdieu, *Distinction,* 66.

47. On the general status of anxiety and loss in economic security of nineteenth-century clerks, see Brian Luskey, *On the Make: Clerks and the Quest for Capital* (New York: New York University Press, 2010).

48. For example, see Crowninshield, *A Private Journal,* 52–58.

49. "Why We Get Sick," 645.

50. Hasia Diner discusses the wonder of the wide availability of meat to Irish, Italian, and Jewish immigrants in *Hungering for America.*

51. Boston baked beans were distinctive because they were made with brown beans, instead of white, and baked with pork. In addition, they were left whole as opposed to other versions, in which the beans were mashed slightly.

52. On the reluctance of some white Bostonians to dine among blacks, see the *Liberator,* January 22, 1831.

53. The *Christian Recorder* reprinted Douglass's 1846 story on June 10, 1886 in "Anniversary Exercises," 1.

54. "Whitman Looks at Boston," *New England Quarterly* 1 (July 1928): 356.

55. John Daniels, *In Freedom's Birthplace: A Study of the Boston Negroes* (Boston: Arno Press, 1914), 94–95. The state legislature passed the law in 1865 and strengthened its provisions the following year. In 1885, the legislature again buttressed the law by broadening it to include unlicensed places of business. See Pleck, *Black Migration and Poverty, Boston 1865–1900* (New York, 1979), 29. Of course, such laws did not mean that discrimination against blacks in restaurants did not occur. Segregation may also have deepened in the early twentieth century, as Boston's black population grew. In 1913, for example, a black who tried to integrate a restaurant faced the possibility of being arrested and fined for disturbing the peace. *Bryant v. Rich's Grill,* 216 Mass. 344 (1912), cited in Perry R. Duis, *The Saloon: Public Drinking in Chicago and Boston 1880–1920* (Chicago: University of Illinois Press, 1983), 336, n. 53.

56. Pleck, *Black Migration and Poverty,* 29.

57. *Acton in America,* 48.

58. Pleck, *Black Migration and Poverty,* 159; John Weiss, *Life and Correspondence of Theodore Parker,* 2 vols. (New York: D. Appleton, 1864), 2:95; Joseph Willard, *A Half a Century with Judges and Lawyers* (Boston: Houghton Mifflin, 1896), 239.

59. Handlin, *Boston's Immigrants,* Table XIII; Carroll D. Wright, *The Census of Massachusetts, 1880* (Boston: Wright & Potter Printing, 1883), 424–25. Unfortunately, it is impossible to determine the specific genre of eatery these immigrants

operated. See also Leonard P. Curry, *The Free Black in Urban America, 1800–1850: The Shadow of a Dream* (Chicago: University of Chicago Press, 1981), 19–20.

60. Abdy quoted in Curry, *Free Black in Urban America*, 19–20.

61. Seventh Census of the United States, 1850, Manuscript Population schedules, Boston City, Suffolk County, Massachusetts.

62. *The Boston Directory, for the Year 1855: Embracing the City Record, a General Directory of the Citizens, and a Business Directory* (Boston: Geo Adams, 1855); Weiss, *Life and Correspondence of Theodore Parker*, 2:95.

63. *Dictionary of American Negro Biography*, Rayford Logan and Michael R. Winston, eds. (New York: Norton, 1982), 565.

64. Ibid.; *Statement of the Claim of the Late Joshua B. Smith against the Commonwealth for Subsistence Furnished the 12th Regiment of Massachusetts Volunteers*, petition (May 14, 1879).

65. Shane White, "Freedoms' First Con: Changing Notes: African Americans and Changing Notes in Antebellum New York City," *Journal of the Early Republic* 34, no 3 (Fall 2014): 385–409.

66. Stephen Mihm, *A Nation of Counterfeiters: Capitalists, Con Men, and the Making of the United States* (Cambridge, Mass.: Harvard University Press, 2007), 1–7, 238.

67. White, "Freedoms' First Con."

68. *Boston Daily Globe*, November 12, 1880, 1.

69. See, for example, "Affairs in and about the City," *Boston Daily Atlas*, February 4, 1854, 2.

70. "He Berated the Cook," *Boston Daily Globe*, April 17, 1890, 8.

71. "Boston's Sandwiches," *Boston Daily Globe*, September 8, 1889, 23.

72. Massachusetts *Acts and Resolves*, 1852, ch. 322. Boston city leadership let the law go flagrantly unenforced in the city's restaurants, however. In 1855, Boston's mayor and alderman mandated that policemen or judges (city employees) who spent time prosecuting offenders of the state's liquor law would have to pay back a portion of their salaries to the city. "Preamble and Resolutions in Relation to Enforcing the Liquor Law," City Doc. No. 40, May 10, 1855. On saloon lunches in Boston, see Duis, *The Saloon*, 52–56. In fact, saloons in Massachusetts were required to offer food in order to sell alcohol.

73. The diners that came to dot northeastern cities beginning in the 1920s were the legacy of eating houses. These venues flourished during Prohibition, which eliminated their competition, the saloons, and welcomed women and children to dine alongside men. Andrew Hurley, "From Hash House to Family Restaurant: The Transformation of the Diner and Post–World War II Consumer Culture," *Journal of American History* 83, no. 4 (March 1997): 1284.

3. CHARLOTTE RUSSE IN THE AFTERNOON

1. Argus, *A Tale of Lowell. Norton; or, the Lights and Shades of a Factory Village: Wherein Are Developed Some of the Secret Incidents in the History of Lowell* (Lowell: Vox Populi Office, 1849), 38–39.

Notes to Chapter 3

2. Ibid.

3. Amal Amireh, *The Factory Girl and the Seamstress: Imagining Gender and Class in Nineteenth-Century American Fiction* (New York: Garland, 2000).

4. Historians Andrew Haley, Cindy Lobel, and Jessica Ellen Sewell also make this point in their respective analyses of women's dining activities: Haley, *Turning the Tables*, 152; Lobel, *Urban Appetites*, 131; Sewell, *Women and the Everyday City*, 94.

5. Historians like Christine Stansell, Mary Ryan, Kathy Peiss, Sarah Deutsch, and Jessica Ellen Sewell have broken new ground in demonstrating the ways women were both present and active in shaping urban space, though this space was gendered as masculine. Stansell, *City of Women: Sex and Class in New York, 1789–1860* (New York: Knopf, 1986); Ryan, *Women in Public: Between Banners and Ballots, 1825–1880* (Baltimore: Johns Hopkins University Press, 1990); Peiss, *Cheap Amusements: Working Women and Leisure in Turn-of-the-Century New York* (Philadelphia: Temple University Press, 1986); Deutsch, *Women and the City: Gender, Space, and Power in Boston, 1870–1940* (New York: Oxford University Press, 2000); Sewell, *Women and the Everyday City*.

6. Cindy Lobel, "Consuming Classes: Changing Food Consumption Patterns in New York City, 1790–1860," Ph.D. diss. (City University of New York, 2003), 123.

7. William Harvard Eliot, *A Description of the Tremont House*, 1.

8. Costard Sly, *Sayings and Doings at the Tremont House in the Year 1832 . . .* , ed. Zachary Philemon Vangrifter, 2 vols. (Boston: Allen and Ticknor, 1833), 1:76.

9. Eliot, *Description of the Tremont House*, 12.

10. For a more detailed gendered reading of space in luxury hotels like the Tremont, see Molly Winger Berger, "A House Divided: Technology, Gender, and Consumption in America's Luxury Hotels, 1825–1860," in *His and Hers: Gender, Consumption, and Technology*, ed. Roger Horowitz and Arwen Mohun (Charlottesville: University Press of Virginia, 1997), 39–65.

11. Eliot, *Description of the Tremont House*, 38–39.

12. Revere House (Boston, Mass.) Records, box 4, book 12, 1879 Inventory, 8 (Massachusetts Historical Society, Boston); John B. Fitzpatrick, *Catalogue: Mammoth Auction Sale, Tremont House . . .* (Boston: Kiley, 1894), 48.

13. The Parker House, for example, redecorated its ladies' dining room in 1866, 1882, and 1887.

14. "Parker's," *Boston Daily Advertiser*, July 6, 1882, 8.

15. Bushman, *The Refinement of America*, 441.

16. *The Housekeepers' Annual and Ladies' Register for 1844* (Boston: J. H. Carter, 1843), 57. Quoted in ibid.

17. Counters would lose their association with bars during Prohibition.

18. Sewell, *Women and the Everyday City*, 82.

19. On the association between contained appetites and refinement, see John Kasson, *Rudeness and Civility*, 195–201.

Notes to Chapter 3

20. J. K. Hoyt, *The Romance of the Table in Three Parts* (New Brunswick, N.J.: Times Publishing, 1872), 33.

21. George Foster, *New York by Gas-Light and Other Urban Sketches,* ed. Stuart Blumin (Berkeley: University of California Press, 1990), 133.

22. As historian Wendy Woloson has demonstrated, by the nineteenth century sugar itself had a strong feminine connotation. Woloson, *Refined Tastes: Sugar, Confectionery, and Consumers in Nineteenth-Century America* (Baltimore: Johns Hopkins University Press, 2002).

23. "Women in a Restaurant," *Boston Daily Globe,* March 18, 1888, 10.

24. "Scenes in a Ladies' Restaurant," *Boston Daily Globe,* December 22, 1889, 24.

25. Murray quoted in Berger, "A House Divided," 51.

26. Whiting, *A Schedule of the Buildings and Their Occupancy*; Perry Duis, *The Saloon,* 186.

27. Bostonians referred to some confectioners as *ice-cream parlors,* though that term did not appear in the city directory.

28. Quoted in Lobel, *Urban Appetites,* 126.

29. J. R. Garcia, "The Ice-Cream Quick Step," sheet music (Boston: J. R. Garcia, 1841), from Library of Congress, Music Copyright Deposits 1820–1860 (http://lcweb2.loc.gov/diglib/ihas/loc.music.sm1841.020950/default.html).

30. *Brown's New Guidebook and Map for Boston* (Boston: H. A Brown, 1872), 93.

31. For an excellent reading of early twentieth-century ladies' eateries, see Sewell, *Women and the Everyday City,* 67–94. On tearooms, see Jan Whitaker, *Tea at the Blue Lantern Inn: A Social History of the Tea Room Craze in America* (New York: St. Martin's, 2002). Cafeterias were mixed-gendered venues but, as Sewell points out, they made themselves respectable for unescorted women to visit by providing separate tables, eliminating alcohol, and creating a light, hygienic décor.

32. Spring, *Boston and the Parker House,* 140–41.

33. Helen R. Deese, ed., *Selected Journals of Caroline Healey Dall, Volume I: 1838–1855* (Boston: Massachusetts Historical Society, 2006), 23.1

34. Helen R. Deese, ed., *Daughter of Boston: The Extraordinary Diary of a Nineteenth-century Woman Caroline Healey Dall* (Boston: Beacon, 2005), 301.

35. Spring, *Boston and the Parker House,* 176.

36. "Scenes in a Ladies' Restaurant," 24.

37. "Women in a Restaurant," 10.

38. "Women in a Restaurant," 10.

39. Kasson, *Rudeness and Civility,* 132.

40. Margaret Sangster, *Good Manners for All Occasions* (New York: Cupples and Leon, 1904), 41.

41. Etiquette manual quoted in Kasson, *Rudeness and Civility,* 132.

42. Marianne Finch, *An Englishwoman's Experience in America* (1853; reprint New York: Negro Universities Press, 1969), 31.

43. Kate Haulman, *The Politics of Fashion in Eighteenth-century America* (Chapel Hill: University of North Carolina Press, 2011), 84–85.

Notes to Chapter 3

44. Tomes, "Before, At, and After Meals," 731. See also "Why We Get Sick," 642–47; Gesner, "Concerning Restaurants," 592.

45. Mrs. J. C. Croly (Jennie June), *Jennie June's American Cookery Book* (New York: American News Company, 1870), 225.

46. "Young Women Order a Luncheon," *Boston Daily Globe*, April 21, 1889, 21; W. D. Howells, *Their Wedding Journey* (Boston: James R. Osgood, 1872), 13; "Women in a Restaurant," 10.

47. "Young Women Order a Luncheon," 21.

48. "Where Women Drink," *Boston Daily Globe*, December 23, 1889, 6; M. A. Avery, "Deciding a Destiny," *Godey's Lady's Book and Magazine* 94 (1877): 69.

49. Cindy Lobel finds evidence of similar anxieties in her study of eating habits in nineteenth-century New York; Foster, *New York by Gas-light*, 134; also quoted in Lobel, *Urban Appetites*, 130.

50. Foster, *New York by Gas-light*, 134.

51. "Ober's Reopening," *Boston Daily Globe*, November 25, 1884, 4.

52. Bushman, *Refinement of America*, 441.

53. It would be well into the next century before these hotels began allowing unescorted women to dine anywhere but in the ladies' dining room.

54. Leslie Dorsey and Janice Devine, *Fare Thee Well: A Backward Look at Two Centuries of Historic American Hostelries, Fashionable Spas & Seaside Resorts* (New York: Crown, 1964), 57.

55. "Dining Out," *Boston Daily Advertiser*, April 5, 1875, 2. See also "Our Ladies," *Harper's New Monthly Magazine* 15, no. 112 (September 1859): 526–29; Richard Grant White, "The Unsociables of Society," *The Galaxy* 8, no. 3 (September 1869): 405–16.

56. Haley, *Turning the Tables*, 151–52.

57. Tunis G. Campbell, *Hotel Keepers, Head Waiters, and Housekeepers' Guide*, 41–42.

58. Most hotels had established mealtimes for servants and children staying at the hotel, suggesting that they were not welcome during the regular dining hours.

59. Quoted in *American Cookery: A Monthly Dining Room Magazine* 1 (September 1876): 145.

60. For example, see Ella Rodman Church, "Money-Making for Ladies," *Harper's New Monthly Magazine* 65, no. 385 (June 1882): 112–16.

61. The Married Women Doing Business Certificates list 340 female commercial eatery proprietors between 1868 and 1891. Sixty-eight are specified as confectioners. Married Women Doing Business Certificates, vols. 1–6, Boston City Archives, Boston.

62. Ninth Census of the United States, 1870, Manuscript Population schedules, Boston City, Suffolk County, Massachusetts.

63. Historian Richard Pillsbury, for example, has found that roughly only 2 percent of the restaurants, oyster houses, and coffeehouses that existed in 1850

136   Notes to Chapter 3

remained open more than ten years. Pillsbury, *From Boarding House to Bistro*, 28. Census data on restaurants were not collected until the late 1920s. Haley, *Turning the Tables*, 269, n. 58.

64. For an example of a credit report of a female restaurateur, see Massachusetts, 13:330, R. G. Dun & Co. Collection, Baker Library, Harvard Business School. On women's petty entrepreneurship in Boston late in the century, see Sarah Deutsch, *Women and the City*, 115–35, esp. 130–32.

65. Daniel E. Sutherland reports that meals were an integral part of domestic servants' wages until the twentieth century. Sutherland, *Americans and Their Servants: Domestic Service in the United States from 1800 to 1920* (Baton Rouge: Louisiana State University Press, 1981), 113.

66. Sewell, *Women and the Everyday City*, 83.

67. Katherine Leonard Turner, *How the Other Half Ate: A History of Working-class Meals at the Turn of the Century* (Berkeley: University of California Press, 2014), 76.

68. Duis, *The Saloon*, 54.

69. Turner, *How the Other Half Ate*, 78; Duis, *The Saloon*, 186.

4. ROAST, CHOP SUEY, AND BEER

1. "Boston's Foreign Restaurants,' *Boston Daily Globe*, January 7, 1894, 24.

2. The number of lodging houses in Boston rose from 289 in 1860 to 741 by 1880, a percent growth of nearly 106. Mark Peel, "On the Margins: Lodgers and Boarders in Boston, 1860–1900," *Journal of American History* 72, no. 4 (March 1986): 818.

3. Albert Benedict Wolfe, *The Lodging House Problem in Boston* (Cambridge, Mass.: Harvard University Press, 1913), 45.

4. Albert Benedict Wolfe would note in his study that a growing trade of "'ready-to-eat' groceries, bread, cake, crackers, cooks, cream and milk, pickles, olives, etc." available from "small bake shops and delicatessen depots" also helped to feed lodgers (ibid., 28).

5. William Dean Howells explains this logic in his novel *A Modern Instance* (1882; reprint, Boston: Houghton Mifflin, 1957), 120–21.

6. Sarah Deutsch, *Women and the City*, 6, 89–90; Michael P. Conzen and George K. Lewis, *Boston: A Geographical Portrait* (Cambridge, Mass.: Ballinger, 1976), 12, 35–37.

7. Mary Antin, *The Promised Land* (Boston: Houghton Mifflin, 1911), 287. Antin was describing the South End, where her family lived, in the 1890s.

8. Andrew Coe, *Chop Suey: A Cultural History of Chinese Food in the United States* (New York: Oxford University Press, 2009), 169. Until 1892, more blacks lived in the West End than anywhere else in the city. But hostility and prejudice within the black community against black southerners, typically former slaves, led southern black migrants to Boston after 1864 to settle disproportionately in the South End. According to Elizabeth Hafkin Pleck, "By 1880, two thirds of all

southern black adults lived in the five wards of the South End, but less than a quarter of blacks from elsewhere resided there." Beginning in 1890, and, more noticeably after 1895, there was a movement to the South End among native black Bostonians as well. See Pleck, *Black Migration and Poverty*, 77; John Daniels, *In Freedom's Birthplace: A Study of the Boston Negroes* (Boston: Houghton Mifflin, 1914), 143.

9. For a table listing the percentage of various nationalities residing in lodging houses in Boston in 1891, see Frederick A. Bushee, *Ethnic Factors in the Population of Boston* (New York: Macmillan, 1903), 27. The decline of the South End reached a tipping point with the financial panic of 1873. Many of the newer homes on Columbia Avenue had been built on mortgages and after the panic hit were owned by banks. The banks sold them for what they could get to people who then rented them out. The remaining wealthy families elsewhere in the South End quickly sold their homes as well, erecting new ones in the fashionable Back Bay. According to one authority, "The people got out of the South End like rats." Wolfe, *Lodging House Problem in Boston*, 14.

10. Deutsch, *Women and the City*, 92; Joanne Meyerowitz, "Sexual Geography and Gender Economy: The Furnished Room Districts of Chicago, 1890–1930," in *Unequal Sisters: An Inclusive Reader in U.S. Women's History*, ed. Vickie L. Ruiz, 4th ed. (New York: Routledge, 2007), 307–23. Pauline Hopkins describes the mixed-gender clientele of an African American lodging house in turn-of-the-century Boston in *Contending Forces: A Romance Illustrative of Negro Life North and South* (1900; reprint, New York: AMS Press, 1971).

11. Many food reformers had long campaigned to shift the main meal later so that it could take place once "the labors of the day are done, when one feels at liberty to unbend, and indulge in pleasant social converse." See, for example, the *Boston Investigator*, September 22, 1847; Robert Tomes, "Before, At, and After Meals," 729–35. Some did worry about the shift, however. See, for example, J. C. Croly, *Jennie June's American Cookery Book*, 225. For more on the shift in mealtimes and the reasons the evening meal became special, see Abigail Carroll, *Three Squares: The Invention of the American Meal* (New York: Basic Books, 2013), 57–76. Boston residents reputedly lagged behind New York in shifting their main meal. *Harper's Bazaar* reported in 1886 that "many people in Boston still dine at two" (quoted in Carroll, *Three Squares*, 62).

12. Sarah Deutsch, for example, found that young working-class women preferred mixed-sex venues to the "girls' clubs" run by reformers (*Women and the City*, 96–97).

13. Kathy Peiss, *Cheap Amusements*; Deutsch, *Women and the City*, 92.

14. Antin offers a lively description of the pushcarts that crowded the South End late in the century in *The Promised Land*, 287.

15. A number of works describe the heterosocial youth culture of the late nineteenth century among the working classes. In Boston, see Deutsch, *Women and the City*.

16. On "treating," see Peiss, *Cheap Amusements*, 53–55.

17. Deutsch, *Women and the City*, 94–98. One "urban legend" that circulated widely in late-nineteenth-century Boston recounted how it was common for a working-class woman to convince a young man to treat for dinner in one of the city's restaurants, leading the young man to believe he would be rewarded through some sexual favor. Instead, once dinner was over, the young woman slipped away, taking her benefactor's wallet along with her. Such tales registered discomfort with the growing presence of unattached single women in commercial venues. For one version of the story, see the *Boston Daily Globe*, October 21, 1882, 2.

18. I formed this impression by consulting the wonderful bill of fare collections at the American Antiquarian Society and the New York Public Library.

19. Wolfe, *Lodging House Problem in Boston*, 27–28.

20. For example, see Massachusetts, vol. 16:20, R. G. Dun & Co. Credit Report Volumes, Baker Business Historical Collections, Harvard Business School, 4:254; 15:511. On the importance of loyalty, see, for example, 11:52.

21. Some female employees also received meals as compensation in addition to their wages. "Boston's Working Women—About the Women Who Work in Restaurants," *Boston Daily Globe*, January 13, 1883, 1. See also *Social Statistics of Working Women, Prepared by the Massachusetts Bureau of Statistics of Labor* (Boston: n.p., 1901), 8, 11–13.

22. On the benefits of employing female waiters over male waiters, see "Priscilla's Difficulties," *Boston Daily Globe*, February 10, 1883, 6; and "Dinner for a Dime," *Boston Daily Globe*, December 24, 1885, 4.

23. "Boston's Working Women," 1.

24. Only three black female waiters appear in the digitized 1880 U.S. manuscript census schedules for Suffolk County, Massachusetts available through ancestry.com (accessed October 13, 2013).

25. Pleck, *Black Migration and Poverty*, 129.

26. Howells, *A Modern Instance*, 121–23.

27. Such a strategy was employed and advertised, for example, at an establishment at 700 Washington. Trade Cards Collection, Box 17, "Cosmopolitan Dining Rooms," Baker Business Historical Collections, Harvard Business School, Boston.

28. Howells, *A Modern Instance*, 121–23.

29. For example, see Menu, "Union Café," the Union Café, Boston, 1876, American Antiquarian Society.

30. Boston's foreign-born population that hailed from parts of the world besides Great Britain grew by 109 percent between 1850 and 1880.

31. Bushee, *Ethnic Factors in the Population of Boston*, 26–27.

32. Jane Ziegelman, *97 Orchard: An Edible History of Five Immigrant Families in One New York Tenement* (New York: Smithsonian Books, 2010), 167.

33. William M. DeMarco, *Ethnics and Enclaves: Boston's Italian North End* (Ann Arbor, Mich: UMI Research Press, 1981), xvi, 1.

Notes to Chapter 4   139

34. On the gastronomic history and culture of Germany, see Christine Metzger, ed., *Culinaria: Germany* (New York: Konemann, 2000).

35. "Boston's Foreign Restaurants," 24.

36. Benjamin Crowninshield, *A Private Journal*, 138, 141.

37. Stephen Puleo, *The Boston Italians: A Story of Pride, Perseverance, and Paesani, from the Years of the Great Immigration to the Present Day* (Boston: Beacon, 2007), xii–xiii.

38. DeMarco, *Ethnics and Enclaves*, 80; Hasia Diner, *Hungering for America*, 79.

39. The descriptions of the Italian café setting are quoted from "Boston's Foreign Restaurants," 24.

40. Coe, *Chop Suey*, 169.

41. "Chinese Cooking," *Boston Daily Globe*, July 19, 1885, 9.

42. "Chinese Restaurants," *Boston Daily Globe*, June 23, 1889, 23.

43. On the foodways of Chinese immigrants in America, see Coe, *Chop Suey*; and Samantha Barbas, "'I'll Take Chop Suey': Restaurants as Agents of Culinary and Cultural Change," *Journal of Popular Culture* 36, no. 4 (May 2003): 669–86.

44. "Boston's Foreign Restaurants," 24.

45. "Advertisement," *Boston Daily Globe*, October 12, 1872. *Curry* was a rather generic English term used to describe a wide variety of dishes with supposed origins in India, but which often had questionable authenticity. This was also the period in which curry powder became a mainstay of grocery store shelves. See *The Dining Room Magazine* 1, no. 12 (December 1876): 197; Kristin L. Hoganson, *Consumers' Imperium: The Global Production of American Domesticity, 1865–1920* (Chapel Hill: University of North Carolina Press, 2007), 108, 114–15.

46. In 1880, Irish immigrants represented about 6 percent of restaurant keepers and 14 percent of male hotel and restaurant employees. Carroll D. Wright, *The Census of Massachusetts, 1880* (Boston: Wright & Potter Printing, 1883), 424–25.

47. Diner, *Hungering for America*, chap. 5.

48. Boston's black community remained overwhelmingly concentrated in low-paying, menial occupations in the late nineteenth century. The digitized 1880 U.S. manuscript census schedules for Suffolk County Massachusetts available through ancestry.com list only three black restaurant keepers (accessed October 13, 2013). Elizabeth Hafkin Pleck has estimated that the 1880 U.S. census underenumerated Boston's black population by a third (*Black Migration and Poverty*, 215). Nevertheless, the number of black restaurant keepers in Boston was undoubtedly low in this period due to the factors discussed in the text. For further discussion of black businesses in Boston late in the century, see ibid., 151–57.

49. Fifty percent of Boston's native black population was born in southern states, according to the 1880 U.S. Census. Pleck, *Black Migration and Poverty*, Table III–1. Although it is exceedingly difficult to determine whether a black Bostonian was a former slave, Pleck concludes that indeed most of the black Southerners in late nineteenth-century Boston had once been slaves (*Black Migration and Poverty*, 54–55).

50. On soul food, see Frederick Douglass Opie, *Hog and Hominy: Soul Food from Africa to America* (New York: Columbia University Press, 2008).

51. Pleck, *Black Migration and Poverty*, 153.

52. Stephan Thernstrom, *The Other Bostonians: Poverty and Progress in the American Metropolis, 1880–1970* (Cambridge, Mass.: Harvard University Press, 1973); Pleck, *Black Migration and Poverty*, 9, 153–57.

53. "Dinner for a Dime," 4.

54. C. W. Gesner, "Concerning Restaurants," *Harper's New Monthly Magazine* 32, no. 191 (April 1866): 593.

55. "Boston's Foreign Restaurants," 24.

56. *Boston Investigator*, January 25, 1854.

57. James E. McWilliams, *A Revolution in Eating*.

58. Hoganson, *A Consumer's Imperium*, 105–51. Andrew Haley argues that this sense of cosmopolitanism gradually overturned the cultural hegemony of the elite French restaurant. See *Turning the Tables*, 92–117.

59. The North and later West Ends were notorious for the prostitution and gambling activities that went on there, while the South End became known for its opium dens. Roger Lane, *Policing the City: Boston, 1822–1885* (New York: Atheneum, 1971); "Wave of Reform," *Boston Daily Advertiser*, July 3, 1899, 1.

60. After 1865, railroads often employed Chinese immigrants. Chinese work gangs included their own Chinese cooks, supplied with special ingredients like sweet rice, dried bamboo sprouts, dried fish, and Chinese sugar. Chinese restaurants also sprang up along the tracks. Coe, *Chop Suey*, 137–38.

61. "Quoe's Guests," *Boston Daily Globe*, March 1, 1891, 4.

62. Howells, *A Modern Instance*, 176.

63. Haley, *Turning the Tables*, 43–67.

64. Historians Andrew Haley, Samantha Barbas, and Andrew Coe all find a new willingness to embrace ethnic cuisine at the turn of the century among the white middle class in cities throughout the nation: ibid., 97; Barbas, "I'll Take Chop Suey," 673–75; Coe, *Chop Suey*, 180–210.

65. "Boston's Foreign Restaurants," 24.

66. "Chinese Cooking," 9.

67. Ibid.

68. For example, see ibid.

69. "Boston's Foreign Restaurants," 24.

70. Ibid.

71. Ibid.

72. Ibid., "Chinese Restaurants," 23.

73. Haley, *Turning the Tables*, 105–108.

74. "Chinese Restaurants," 23.

75. Ibid.

76. Coe, *Chop Suey*, 60.

77. Barbas, "I'll Take Chop Suey," 674.

Notes to Chapter 4

78. "In the New Chinatown," *Boston Daily Globe,* July 13, 1894, 1.

79. "Quoe's Guests," 4.

80. "Boston's Foreign Restaurants," 24.

81. Hoganson, *Consumers' Imperium,* 21–22.

82. Jessica Ellen Sewell, *Women and the Everyday City;* the *Boston Daily Globe* reported on the perceived threat of restaurants loosening codes of behavior among women (December 23, 1889, 6). Likewise, William Dean Howells describes respectable middle-class white women in German beer halls. Early editions even included an image of the middle-class female heroine drinking a beer, as shown in figure 28 (Howells, *Their Wedding Journey,* 107–109, image on 108).

83. On slumming, see Chad Heap, *Slumming: Sexual and Racial Encounters in American Nightlife, 1885–1940* (Chicago: University of Chicago Press, 2010).

84. "Many Complaints," *Boston Daily Advertiser,* July 4, 1899, 2. See also "Wave of Reform," 1.

85. "Boston's Foreign Restaurants," 24.

86. Ibid. On other cities' sense of civic pride regarding their range of ethnic restaurants at the turn of the century, see Hoganson, *Consumers' Imperium,* 117.

87. On food as a cultural bridge, see Barbas, "'I'll Take Chop Suey.'"

88. See, for example, "Two Song Assaulted: A Harrison Ave Chinamen Struck by a Brick," *Boston Daily Globe,* September 17, 1889, 1; "The Heathen Chinese," *Boston Daily Globe,* December 23, 1877.

89. Lisa Heldke, *Exotic Appetite: Ruminations of a Food Adventurer* (New York: Routledge, 2003), xvi.

90. Barbas, "'I'll Take Chop Suey,'" 683.

91. Boston's Chinese population was relatively small anyway—just 121 Chinese were counted in Boston in 1880. Handlin, *Boston's Immigrants,* 213.

92. Joseph Conforti, *Imagining New England: Explorations of Regional Identity from the Pilgrims to the Mid-twentieth Century* (Chapel Hill: University of North Carolina Press, 2000), chap. 5.

93. Harvey Levenstein, "The New England Kitchen and the Origins of Modern American Eating Habits," *American Quarterly* 32, no. 4 (Autumn 1980): 369–86.

94. Laura Shapiro, *Perfection Salad: Women and Cooking at the Turn of the Century* (New York: Farrar, Straus, and Giroux, 1986), 48.

95. Ibid., 148.

96. Katherine Leonard Turner also makes this point in *How the Other Half Ate,* 114.

97. Robert Woods, ed., *Americans in Process: A Settlement Study* (Boston: Houghton, Mifflin, 1903), 142; Croly, *Jennie June's American Cookery Book,* 225; Duis, *The Saloon,* 108.

98. Turner, *How the Other Half Ate,* 134.

99. Ellen Richards, "Scientific Cooking: Studies in the New England Kitchen," *Forum* 15 (May 1893): 355–59. Quoted in Levenstein, "The New England Kitchen,"

142   Notes to Chapter 4

375. Katherine Leonard Turner also explores the complicated stance that the developers of the New England Kitchen, particularly Ellen Richards, took on consumerism and food. She points out that in later years home economists like Christine Frederick would begin to work closely with food manufacturers to promote easier cooking and housekeeping. These reformers continued to disapprove of dining out but embraced mass-produced, commercial foods eaten at home as a compromising solution to keep women at their stoves (albeit for less time) and families around the domestic dinner table. See Turner, *How the Other Half Ate,* 135.

100. Fannie Merritt Farmer's *Boston Cooking-School Cookbook,* however, did contain several foreign recipes, including "Spanish Omelet," "Sauce Á l'Italienne," and spaghetti. Fannie Merritt Farmer, *The Boston Cooking-School Cookbook* (Boston: Little, Brown, 1896).

101. Hoganson, *Consumers' Imperium,* 149.

102. Donna Gabaccia, *We Are What We Eat: Ethnic Food and the Making of Americans* (Cambridge, Mass.: Harvard University Press, 2000), chap. 3; Hoganson, *Consumers' Imperium,* chap. 3; Haley, *Turning the Tables,* chap. 4; Sewell, *Women and the Everyday City,* chap. 3.

103. Haley, *Turning the Tables,* 115.

EPILOGUE

1. Anthony Mitchell Sammarco, *Howard Johnson's: How a Massachusetts Soda Fountain Became an American Icon* (Charleston, S.C.: History Press, 2013), 17–18.

2. Ibid.

3. Ibid., 18–20.

4. Andrew Hurley, "From Hash House to Family Restaurant: The Transformation of the Diner and Post–World War II Consumer Culture," *Journal of American History* 83, no. 4 (March 1997): 1284.

Index

Abdy, Edward, 59
abolitionists, in Boston, 34, 59
Acton, Sir John, 29
advertising: by confectioners, 70, 71, 76–77; by Howard Johnson's, 109
African Americans: in Boston, xv–xvii, 136–37n8; cooks, 60; discrimination against, xiii, xix, 58, 59–60, 84, 87–88, 94, 131n55; neighborhoods, xvii, 84, 94, 136–37n8; racial tensions, 60; restaurant owners, 59–60, 94, 139n48; soul food, 94; southern migrants, 136–37n8, 139n49; waiters, xix, 28–29, 30, 31, 32–34, 58–59, 88; women, 87–88; workers, xiii, 117n18. *See also* slaves
Agassiz, Louis, 72
alcohol: association with commercial sex, 2, 65; bans, 61; food served with, 61, 78, 86, 132n72; German beer halls, 141n82; hotel bars, 78; not sold in ladies' dining rooms, 69, 75; sellers, 46, 48, 81, 129n9, 132n72; served in ethnic cafés, 90, 91, 98, 100; served in hotel dining rooms, 25, 41, 78; women drinking, 100, 141n82. *See also* taverns
American Frugal Housewife, The (Child), 27

American House, 36, 63, 76
American Physiological Society, xxi
Andrew, John, 59

Barbas, Samantha, 102
beans, baked: Boston, 57–58, 89, 131n51; served in eating houses, 48, 53, 57–58; served in hotel dining rooms, 24; as traditional food, 102
beer. *See* alcohol
bills of fare: of cafés, 88, 89; distinction from menus, 123n66; of eating houses, 46, 53; French dishes, 41; of hotel dining rooms, 20, 21, 22, 24–25, 26, 41–42; ordering from, 41
Blot, Pierre, 125n93
boardinghouses, xiii, 84, 116–17n16
Boardman, James, 14, 35
Boston: cultural influence, xx, 9–12; downtown commercial district, 45–46, 65; French Revolution celebrations, 23; interest in food, xx–xxi; manufacturing and industry, xi, xvii, 10; mayors, 1, 28; physical expansion, xi, xiv, 117nn21–22; population growth, xi, xiv, 117n21; suburbs, xiv, xvii, 117n21; visitors, xi–xii, 6, 12, 29. *See also* Boston maps

143

Boston Atlas, 52
Boston Cooking School, xxi, 102–3,
110, 142n100
Boston Courier, 36
Boston Daily Advertiser, 39–40
Boston Daily Globe, 29, 40, 51, 53, 60,
69, 75, 83, 91, 96, 97–98, 100
Boston Herald, 52
Boston Investigator, 95
Boston maps: 1807, x; 1841, xiv; 1856,
xv; 1886, xvi; commercial district,
45; density of dining venues (1850),
66; South Boston, 85; Tremont
House location, 17
Bourdieu, Pierre, 122n39
Boyden, Dwight, 14, 20
Bradford, Thomas G., Boston, xiv
Brigham's, 63
Brillat-Savarin, Jean Anthelme, 120n14
Britain: class differences, 8
Bufford, J. H., "The Breakfast Bell
Polka," 19
Bushman, Richard, 10, 34
business owners, women, 80, 128n5.
See also credit; restaurant owners

cafés: à la carte dishes, 88; bills of
fare, 88, 89; clients, xxiii, 83–85;
counter service, 88; hours, 83;
locations, 86; number of, 83; prices,
86–87, 88–89, 90, 91, 92; table
d'hôte meals, 88–89, 90; tableware,
88; waiter girls, 87–88, 138n21. See
also ethnic cafés
cafeterias, 72, 134n31
Cambridge, Lyon's Oyster Saloon, ix
Campbell, A. R., 54
Campbell, Tunis Galic: Hotel Keepers,
Head Waiters, and Housekeepers'
Guide, 31, 33, 79; portrait, 32
capitalism. See consumer culture
Carr's Eating House, 53
chefs: earnings, 125n98; French, 21–
23; training, 28, 125n93. See also
cooks

Child, Lydia Marie, The American
Frugal Housewife, 27
children: child care, 73, 79; in ethnic
cafés, 90; meals in hotel dining
rooms, 135n58
Chinatown, 84, 96, 100
Chinese cafés: Americanization,
98–99; Chinese customers, 89, 99;
chopsticks, 93, 98; as culinary
adventures, xix, 96, 97–98; decor
and atmosphere, 91–92, 99;
employees, 100–101; food served,
92–93, 95, 96, 97–98, 99
Chinese Exclusion Act, xix, 95, 102
Chinese food: in cafés, 92–93, 95, 96,
97–98, 99; popularity in America,
xix, 102; for railroad workers,
140n60
Chinese immigrants: eating with
chopsticks, 93, 98; hostility toward,
101, 102; immigration laws, xix, 102;
neighborhoods, xvii, 84, 100;
opium dens, 100; workers, xi,
140n60
chopsticks, 93, 98
chop suey, 98, 99
civic organizations: of men, xi–xii, 35;
of women, xii, xxii, 65, 72
civil rights laws, 58, 131n55
Civil War, 59, 60
classes: cultural capital, 122n39; lowest, xiii–xiv, xv, 102–3; mobility, xiii–
xiv, 56; segmentation of dining,
xxii, 41, 44, 110; stratification, xiii–
xvii, 11–12. See also elites; middle
class; workers
colonial period, commercial dining
in, x
Colonial Revival Movement, 102
Colton, G. W.: Boston and Adjacent
Cities (1886), xvi; Map of Boston and
Adjacent Cities (1856), xv
commercial dining: in colonial
period, x; demand for, xi–xiii,
83–86; as entertainment, xii–xiii,

Index

xviii, 84–86; in Europe, 4, 5, 25, 120n12; failure rates, 80, 94, 135–36n63; increased access, ix–xi, xviii–xix; number of establishments, 83, 84, 116n12; segmentation, xiii, xvii, xviii, 64, 110; shift to, x–xiii, xvii–xviii, 105; social relationships and, 108–10. *See also* cafés; confectioners; eating houses; hotel dining rooms; ladies' dining rooms; restaurants; taverns

confectioners: advertising, 70, 71, 76–77; clientele, ix, 79; locations, 70. *See also* ladies' dining rooms

conspicuous consumption, 11, 39, 65, 77

consumer culture, xviii, 11, 104, 108, 110

Contrast, The (Tyler), 31

cooking: American, 24, 26; at eating houses, 48–49; English recipes, 7; home-cooked meals, 74–75, 102–3, 141–42n99. *See also* Boston Cooking School; foods; French cuisine

cooks: African American, 29, 60; immigrants, 29; turnover, 125n100. *See also* chefs

cosmopolitanism, 95, 101, 140n58

counters: association with bars, 68, 133n17; in cafés, 88; in eating houses, 51, 68

Crawford House, 78

credit: for African Americans, 60, 94; ratings of café owners, 86–87; for women business owners, 80

Crowninshield, Benjamin W., ix, xviii, 57

cuisine. *See* cooking; French cuisine

culinary schools, 125n93. *See also* Boston Cooking School

cultural capital, 56, 122n39

cultural imperialism, 101–2

Dall, Caroline Healey, 72

delicatessens, 86, 136n4

Delmonico's, 36, 127n117

Description of the Tremont House, A (Eliot), 15

Deutsch, Sarah, 84

Dickens, Charles, 14, 18–20

Diner, Hasia, 93–94

diners, 132n73

dining à la Russe, 20

dinners. *See* meals

domestic servants. *See* servants

Douglass, Frederick, 58

eating houses: aromas, 50–51, 54; bills of fare, 46, 49, 53; clientele, 43–44, 48, 50, 54, 56–58, 86; competition, 46; decline, 61; dishes served, 48–49, 53, 57–58; distinctions among, xxii, 44, 50–56, 57; emergence, 44; as family businesses, 46, 51, 128n5; female proprietors, 128n5; fires in, 50; furnishings, 51, 54; hours, 44, 46; licenses, 46, 47; locations, 45–46, 50–51, 65, 66; as male spaces, xxii, 44–45, 65, 81; middle-class, 53–56; napkin racks, 54; need for, 43–44; opening, 46; prices, 46, 50, 53, 54, 56; quality of meals, 49, 53, 54, 57–58; racial discrimination, 58; shared experiences, 56–58, 60–61; social change and, 56–57, 61; speed of dining, 46–48, 49, 54; tables, 51; violence among diners and staff, 52, 60; waiters, 51–53, 58–59, 60, 87; women allowed in, 81

Eliot, William Harvard, 12–13, 15–16, 122n47

elites: cultural power, 10–12; dining experiences, 1–2, 39–41, 96–97, 127n123; displays of wealth, 11; eating at ethnic cafés, 96; gender ideals, 64, 74–75; interest in French cuisine, ix, xii–xiii, xxi–xxii, 23–24, 26–27, 96; movement to suburbs, xiv, xvii; prosperity, 10, 11; women,

64, 67–68, 72–73, 77–78. *See also* hotel dining rooms; ladies' dining rooms; refinement

entrepreneurs. *See* business owners; restaurant owners

ethnic cafés: alcohol served in, 90, 91, 100; Americanization, 98–99; as culinary adventures, xxiii, 95–100, 103–4; cultural imperialism and, 101–2; decor and atmosphere, 99–100; diversity, 83, 89–94, 101, 104; German, 89–90, 95, 100; immigrant customers, xiii, 89–91, 98, 99; increased number of, 83; inter-actions with foreigners, 100–101; Italian, 89, 90–91, 95, 98, 101; native-born clients, 83, 94–102, 103–4; newspaper articles on, 94–95, 97–98, 99, 100–101; regional cuisines, 89; tableware, 98–99; waiters, 102. *See also* Chinese cafés

ethnic foods: criticism of, 102–4; curry, 93, 139n45; grocery stores, 91; Italian, 91, 95, 98; popularity in twentieth century, 105. *See also* Chinese food

ethnic groups: enclaves, xvii, 84, 89–93, 100; Irish Americans, 87; regional identities, 89; stereotypes of, 95; of waiters, 52. *See also* Chinese immigrants; immigrants; Irish immigrants

etiquette guides, 26, 40–41, 73. *See also* manners

Europe: commercial dining, 4; table-ware, 7–8; tipping customs, 31; visitors from, 4, 7–8, 14, 29, 35, 48. *See also* France

Everett, Edward, 1–2

Exchange Hotel, 6, 12, 13, 23–24

Farrar, Eliza, *The Young Lady's Friend*, 26

femininity: decor of ladies' dining

rooms, 67–68; luxury and, 9, 10, 35–36, 77

Finch, Marianne, 74

food reformers, xxi, 102–4, 110, 137n11, 141–42n99

foods: Anglo-American, 4, 23–24, 94; baked beans, 24, 48, 53, 57–58, 89, 102, 131n51; in cafés, 88, 89; at eating houses, 48–49, 53, 57–58; hash, 53; in ladies' dining rooms, 69; meat, 48, 53, 89, 129n17; of New England, 7, 89, 102–3; soul food, 94. *See also* bills of fare; cook-ing; ethnic foods; meals

forks, 8, 11, 26, 124n83

France: American interest in culture, 23–24; hotels, 4, 120n12; restaurants, 4, 5, 20, 25, 120n12; Revolution, 4, 9, 23. *See also* French cuisine

franchise restaurants, 108

Franklin, Benjamin, 27

French chefs, 21–23, 28

French cuisine: competition from other ethnic cuisines, 105; elite interest, ix, xii–xiii, xxi–xxii, 23–24, 26–27, 96; at Julien's Restorator, 6, 23; ordering from bill of fare, 41; status, 39, 95; at Tremont House, 1, 21–23, 24–25, 26–27

French Revolution, 4, 9, 23

Fugitive Slave Act, 34. *See also* slaves

gender. *See* femininity; male spaces; masculinity; men; mixed-gender dining; women

gender ideals: challenges to, 74–76, 86; home economics movement and, 103; upheld in ladies' dining rooms, 64. *See also* separate-sphere ideology

German cafés, 89–90, 95, 100

German immigrants, xi, 90, 100, 115–16n10

Gleason's Pictorial, 14–15

Index

Gori, Ferdinando, 21–23, 24
Graham, Sylvester, xxi
grocery stores, ethnic, 91

Haley, Andrew P., 97
Hall, Margaret, 8
Harper's New Monthly Magazine, 50, 95
Harvard University, Class Day, ix
headwaiters, 31. *See also* waiters
Heldke, Lisa, 101
heterosocial youth culture, 84,
    137n12
Hoganson, Kristin L., 95, 104
home economics movement, 102–4,
    141–42n99
hotel dining rooms: bells, 18–20;
    clientele, 4, 7, 39–40; early, 3–4, 6;
    as elite experience, 39–42, 96–97,
    127n123; exclusion of women,
    35–36, 65; kitchen staff, 29; for
    ladies, 35, 67–70, 72, 73, 74, 79; lux-
    ury, 15–17, 27, 36, 39–40, 77; meals
    for children and servants, 135n58;
    meals served, 3–4, 110; mixed-
    gender dining, 63, 77–78; quality
    of meals, 4, 6; table sizes, 16, 20,
    38–39, 77–78; waiters, 28–33, 39–40,
    87. *See also* Parker House Hotel;
    Tremont House
*Hotel Keepers, Head Waiters, and
    Housekeepers' Guide* (Campbell), 31,
    33, 79
hotels: bars, 78; clientele, 67; early,
    3–4, 5–6; employees, 28; European
    Plan, 36–38; in France, 4, 120n12; in
    New York City, 126n115
housing: boardinghouses, xiii, 84,
    116–17n16; in Boston, xiii, xv–xvii;
    lodging houses, 83–84, 136n2; racial
    segregation, 84; slums, xv–xvii; in
    South End, 84, 137n9
Howard Johnson's, 107–8, 109
Howells, William Dean: *A Modern
    Instance,* 88, 89, 96; *Their Wedding
    Journey,* 30, 38, 90

ice-cream parlors. *See* confectioners;
    Howard Johnson's
"The Ice-Cream Quick Step" sheet
    music, 70, 71
immigrants: assimilation, xxi, 103, 104;
    attitudes toward, xiii, xix, 95, 101,
    102; in Boston, xi, xiii, xv, xvii, 115–
    16n10, 138n30; chefs, 23–25, 28;
    cooks and waiters, 28–29, 31, 52–53,
    58, 139n46; economic and social
    mobility, xxiii, 99, 103; German, xi,
    90, 100, 115–16n10; housing, xv;
    Italian, xi, 89, 90–91, 98, 115–16n10;
    meals at eating houses, 57–58;
    meals at ethnic cafés, xiii, 89–91, 95,
    99; restaurant owners, xxiii, 59, 89,
    93–94, 139n46; women, 102–3. *See
    also* Chinese immigrants; ethnic
    groups; Irish immigrants
immigration laws, xix, 95, 102
industrialization, x–xi, xvii, 11, 39
inns, 2, 4. *See also* taverns
Irish Americans, waiter girls, 87
Irish immigrants: in Boston, xi, xiii,
    xvii, 115–16n10; fights with blacks,
    60; restaurant owners, 93–94,
    139n46; starvation in Ireland, 93–94;
    waiter girls, 87; waiters, 28–29, 31,
    52–53, 58, 139n46; workers, xi, 50,
    117n18
Italian cafés, 89, 90–91, 95, 98, 101
Italian immigrants: in Boston, xi, 115–
    16n10; in cafés, 98; neighborhoods,
    xvii, 89, 90–91; regional origins, 89

Jefferson, Thomas, 9, 23
Johnson, Howard Deering, 107–8
Journeymen Ship Carpenters and
    Caulkers of Boston, 43
Julien (Jean Baptiste Gilbert Payplat),
    5, 23, 120n14
Julien's Restorator, 5, 23, 110, 120n14

knives: eating with, 8, 26, 124n83;
    manufacturing processes, 11

labor. *See* servants; unions; waiters; workers

ladies' dining rooms: advertising, 76–77; anxieties associated with, 73–76, 77; clientele, 67–68, 72–73, 76–77, 78–79; criticism of women's behavior, 75–76; desserts, 69; evening meals, 73; female proprietors, 79–80; feminine design elements, 67–68; freestanding, 70–72, 73; gender ideals upheld in, 64; in hotels, 35, 67–70, 72, 73, 74, 79; locations, 70; male guests, 69–70, 75–76; menus, 69; pleasurable gregariousness, 72–73; prices, 79; seating arrangements, 68–69; separate entrances, 67; waiters, 69, 79. *See also* confectioners

Lafayette, Marquis de, 23–24

Lee's ice cream saloon, 70, 71

leisure activities, xii–xiii, xviii, 84–86

Levine, Lawrence, 39

Life magazine, 109

liquor licenses, 129n9, 132n72. *See also* alcohol

Locke-Ober Restaurant, 127n120

lodging houses, 83–84, 136n2

Lowell millworkers, 63–64

Luckey, John, 52

lunch, 61, 86

luxury: criticism of, 27; feminizing effects, 9, 10, 35–36, 77; in hotel dining rooms, 15–17, 27, 36, 39–40, 77; material culture of dining, 7–8

Lyon's Oyster Saloon, Cambridge, ix

MacReady, William Charles, 25

male spaces, xxii, 44–45, 65, 81. *See also* eating houses; hotel dining rooms

manners: American, 7, 9, 26, 124n83; etiquette guides, 26, 40–41, 73; lack of, 4, 7, 48; refined, 12, 40–41

maps. *See* Boston maps

markets. *See* consumer culture

Marshall, John, *Boston et Ses Environs,* x

masculinity: of business, 35; drinking and smoking, 35; of eating houses, xxii, 44–45, 65; effeminate luxury and, 10, 35–36, 77; ideology of refinement and, 35. *See also* male spaces

Massachusetts: alcohol bans, 61; civil rights laws, 58, 131n55; manufacturing, xi; victualling licenses, 47

Massachusetts Anti-Slavery Society, 72

Massachusetts Charitable Mechanics Association, 28

material culture of dining, 7–8. *See also* tableware

meals: French style of service, 20; main meal shifted to evening, 61, 81, 84–85, 137n11; plate dinners, 49; table d'hôte service, 4, 7, 20, 88–89, 90. *See also* cooking; foods

meat: avoiding, 129n17; beef, 48; served at cafés, 89; spoiled, 53

men: civic organizations, xi–xii, 35; guests in ladies' dining rooms, 69–70, 75–76. *See also* male spaces; masculinity; mixed-gender dining

menus: distinction from bills of fare, 123n66; in ladies' dining rooms, 69. *See also* bills of fare

middle class: in cafés, 96; eating houses for, 53–56; in elite dining rooms, 41; expansion, xiii; food reformers, 102–4; gender ideals, 64; interest in ethnic foods, 96, 97–101, 103–4, 140n64; leisure activities, 85–86; white-collar workers, 54; women, xii, 79–80, 141n82

millworkers, 63–64

Minkins, Shadrach, 32–34

minority groups. *See* African Americans; ethnic groups; immigrants

mixed-gender dining: in eating houses, 81; in hotel dining rooms,

63, 77–78; in ladies' dining rooms, 69–70, 75–76. *See also* cafés
Modern Instance, A (Howells), 88, 89, 96
Monroe, James, 6
Morse, John, 52
Murray, Charles August, 14, 70

National Police Gazette, 52
New England foods, 7, 89, 102–3
New England Kitchen, xxi, 103, 110, 141–42n99
New England Watch & Ward Society, 107
New York City: hotels, 126n115; restaurants, xx, 36, 127n117
Nichols, Malcolm, 107
North End, Boston, xiv, xv, 89, 90–91, 102–3, 140n59

Ober, Louis, 97, 127n120
Ober's Restaurant Parisian Café, 97, 127n120
O'Connell's eating house, 60
O'Neill, Eugene, *Strange Interlude,* 107
opium trade, 100, 140n59
oysters, ix, 25, 63, 69

Paris restaurants, 25. *See also* France
Parker, Harvey, 36, 72
Parker House Hotel: bill of fare, 41–42; dining at, ix, 41–42, 110, 128n133; Douglass as guest, 58; European Plan, 36–38; exterior view, 37; ladies' dining room, 67, 68, 72; opening, 36; prices, 41–42, 96–97; restaurant, 36–39; waiters, 40
Payplat, Jean Baptiste Gilbert. *See* Julien
Penniman, John Ritto, *Conflagration of the Exchange Coffee House,* 13
Pillsbury, Richard, 46
Pleck, Elizabeth Hafkin, 58, 94
Power, Tyrone, 25

public dining establishments. *See* cafés; commercial dining; eating houses; hotel dining rooms; ladies' dining rooms; restaurants; taverns
public sphere: male, 65; restaurants as part of, xviii; women in, xxii, 64, 74

Quincy (Massachusetts), Howard Johnson's, 107–8
Quincy, Josiah, 1, 28

race. *See* African Americans; ethnic groups; whites
refinement: criticism of, 25–27; ideology of, 10–12, 18, 27, 34, 35, 122n39; women's appetites, 69. *See also* manners
reformers. *See* food reformers
Reinhart, Charles Stanley, "The Lunch Counter," 49
republicanism: egalitarianism, 8–9, 26, 30–32; refinement and, 11–12, 25–27
restaurant owners: African American, 59–60, 94, 139n48; earnings, 86–87; immigrants, xxiii, 59, 89, 94, 139n46; white, 59; women, 79–80, 128n5. *See also* ethnic cafés
restaurants: in France, 4, 5, 20, 25, 120n12; franchises, 108; Julien's Restorator, 5, 23, 110, 120n14; Locke-Ober, 127n120; as male eating spaces, 65; in New York City, xx, 36, 127n117; racial segregation, 131n55; Tremont Restaurant, 36. *See also* cafés; commercial dining; French cuisine; hotel dining rooms; ladies' dining rooms; waiters
Revere House, 36, 67, 74
Rogers, Isaiah, 13, 15, 126n115

Salmon, Robert, *View of Boston Harbor,* xii
saloons: decor, 68; free lunches, 61, 86, 132n72

150 Index

sandwich shops, 61
separate-sphere ideology, 86, 103.
  See also gender ideals; public
  sphere
servants: meals in hotel dining
  rooms, 135n58; meals provided by
  employer, 136n65; women, xi, 80,
  87, 116n13, 117n18, 136n65
Sewell, Jessica Ellen, 68–69
silver. *See* tableware
slaves: former, 94, 136–37n8, 139n49;
  fugitive, 32–34, 59
Smith, Joshua Bowen, 59
social and civic organizations: of
  men, 35; of women, xii, xxii, 65, 72
social classes. *See* classes
South End, Boston: black population,
  84, 94, 136–37n8; Chinatown, 84, 96,
  100; ethnic cafés, 89, 90; housing,
  84, 137n9; opium dens, 100, 140n59;
  plan, 85; working-class population,
  xvii
Story, Joseph, 1
street vendors, 43, 61, 81, 86

table d'hôte service, 4, 7, 20, 88–89, 90
tableware: American compared to
  European, 7–8; at cafés, 88; chopsticks, 93, 98; at eating houses, 51,
  54; at ethnic cafés, 98–99; in hotel
  dining rooms, 17, 20–21; knives and
  forks, 8, 11, 26, 124n83; manufacturing processes, 11; specialized, 11
Tale of Lowell, A (Argus), 63–64, 76
taverns: clientele, x, 3, 7, 120n6; in
  England, 4; as male spaces, 65;
  meals served, 2–3; regulations, 2–3
tearooms, 72
Their Wedding Journey (Howells), 30,
  38, 90
Thenrstrom, Stephan, 94
tipping, 31, 39–40, 125–26n102
tradesmen, 28. *See also* workers
Tremont House: bills of fare, 20, 21,
  22, 24–25, 26; closing, 42; competi-

tors, 36; construction, xxi–xxii, 1–2,
  13, 28, 110, 122n49; costs of dining
  and lodging, 25; decline, 42; dining
  room, xxii, 1, 2, 15–20, 35, 42;
  elitism, 2, 15–16, 25–27, 34; exterior
  views, 14, 16; financing, 13; French
  chef, 21–23, 24, 28; French cuisine,
  1, 21–23, 24–25, 26–27; furnishings
  and decor, 16–17; gong, 18–20;
  hotel, 13–15, 25; important visitors,
  14, 126n110; influence, 2, 15, 26–27;
  innovations, 13–14, 122n47, 122n49,
  123n58; ladies' dining room, 35,
  67–68, 72; location, 15, 17; luxury,
  xxii, 15–17, 27, 35–36; management,
  14; masculine behaviors, 35–36;
  meals as performances, 18–21, 30;
  opening dinners, 1–2, 28; plans,
  12–13; political and business functions held, 35; quality of meals,
  25; rituals, 18–20; supporters, 27;
  waiters, 1, 20–21, 28–29, 30–31
Tremont Restaurant, 36
Tremont Street, 15, 16, 67, 102
Tremont Theatre, 15, 16
Tudor, Henry, 35
Tyler, Royall, *The Contrast,* 31

unions, 43, 58–59
urban culture, xviii, 105

Veblen, Thorstein, 39
victuallers, 4, 46, 47
Vigne, Godfrey T., 14

waiter girls, 87–88, 138n21
waiters: African American, xix, 28–29,
  30, 31, 32–34, 58–59, 88; clothing, 31;
  dignity, 30–31, 34; in eating houses,
  51–53, 58–59, 60, 87; in ethnic cafés,
  102; ethnicities, 52; in Europe, 31;
  European visitors on, 29; head-, 31;
  in hotel dining rooms, 28–33, 39–40,
  87; immigrants, 28–29, 31, 52–53, 58,
  139n46; ranks, 31; slang, 53; strikes,

58; tipping, 31, 39–40, 125–26n102; training, 31; treatment by customers, 31–34; unions, 58–59; wages, 31, 51, 87
Waiters' Benevolent Association, 58–59
wealthy. *See* elites
Webster, Daniel, 1, 28
Webster, Noah, 8, 9
West End, Boston, xiv, xvii, 84, 136n8, 140n59
Whig party, 8, 10, 27
White, Shane, 59–60
Whitehead, Jessup, 123n66
whites: attitudes toward immigrants, xiii, 95, 101, 102; at ethnic cafés, 83, 94–102, 103–4; fugitive slaves and, 59; inequality, xiii, xiv; interest in ethnic foods, xix, 94–102, 140n64; poor, xvii; racial tensions, 60; restaurant owners, 59; waiter and cook jobs avoided by, 28, 31, 52, 125n96; waiter girls, 87; waiters, xix; xenophobia, 102. *See also* elites; Irish immigrants; middle class
Whitman, Walt, 58
Wiggin, Charles H., 25, 41–42, 128n133
wine. *See* alcohol
Wm. H. Ladd's Eating House, No. 1, Lindall St., Boston, 55
Wolfe, Albert Benedict, 83
women: African American, 87–88; business owners, 80, 128n5; café meals, 86; child care, 73, 79; as consumers, xxii, 65, 77; cooking classes, 102–3; domestic workers, xi, 80, 87, 116n13, 117n18, 136n65;

drinking alcohol, 100, 141n82; in eating houses, 81; elite, 64, 67–68, 72–73, 77–78; employment, xii, 28, 44, 65, 80–81, 86, 116n13; at ethnic cafés, 100; home-cooked meals, 74–75, 102–3, 141–42n99; in hotel dining rooms, 63, 77–78; in lodging houses, 84; nonelite, 63–64, 78–81; respectability, 64, 67, 70, 73, 75–76, 78–79; restaurant owners, 79–80, 128n5; single, 84, 86, 137n12, 138n17; social and civic organizations, xii, xxii, 65, 72; taverns avoided by, 2, 65; tavern keepers' wives, 3; wages, 87; waiter girls, 87–88, 138n21; working-class, 63–64, 80–81. *See also* femininity; ladies' dining rooms; mixed-gender dining
Women's Education Association, 102
workers: African American, xiii, 117n18; cooks, 29, 60, 125n100; eating at ethnic cafés, 95–96; housing, xv, 83–84; immigrants, xi, xv, 117n18, 140n60; industrial, xi, xvii; Irish, xiii, 50, 117n18; lack of mobility, xiii; mechanics, 1, 28; midday dinners, xii, 43, 50–51; time available for meals, 43, 54, 84–86; unions, 43, 58–59; wages, 29, 31; white-collar, 54. *See also* eating houses; servants; waiters
working-class women, 63–64, 80–81

xenophobia, 95, 101. *See also* immigrants

Young Lady's Friend, The (Farrar), 26

KELLY ERBY is assistant professor of history at Washburn University in Topeka, Kansas.